THE NEED FOR HEROES

THE NEED FOR HEROES

BLACK INTELLECTUALS DIG UP THEIR PAST

Edited by Sabrina Gledhill

Editora **Funmilayo** Publishing

Crediton, UK, 2024

Cover design by Miriã Santos Araújo

Cover photo and frontispiece: Memorial to the 54th Massachusetts
Regiment by Augustus Saint-Gaudens (detail). National Gallery,
Washington, D.C. Photo by Sabrina Gledhill, 2013.

Back cover photo: Statue of Zumbi dos Palmares in Praça da Sé,
Salvador, Bahia, Brazil, 2013. Photo by Maurício Tesserolli.
Reproduced with permission from the photographer.

…when he was older and came to know of Frederick Douglass and Toussaint L'Ouverture, he knew if he could but burst his bonds he, too, could write his name in glory.

—Jessie Redmon Fauset, *There is Confusion* (1924)

We know we are not weak, ignorant, frustrated, or cowed. We know the race has its heroes whether anybody puts them into books or not. We know we are heroes ourselves and can make a better world. Someday there will be many books and plays and songs that say that. Today there are strangely few. Negro literature has a need for heroes. Then it will come alive, speak, sing, and flame with meaning for the Negro people.

—Langston Hughes, "The Need for Heroes" (1941)

This book is dedicated to my daughters,
Barbara Cristiane and Isis Maria,
and my grandsons,
Gabriel and John Benjamin

CONTENTS

Foreword: The Negro Digs Up His Past   i
by Arthur A. Schomburg

Editor's Introduction   ix
by Sabrina Gledhill

1   William Cooper Nell   1
   ❖ From *The Colored Patriots of the American
      Revolution*
      o   Crispus Attucks /1

2   George Washington Williams   7
   ❖ *Negroes as Soldiers*
      o   The American War of Independence /7
      o   The U.S. Civil War /12

3   Manuel R. Querino   17
   ❖ *The African Contribution to Brazilian
      Civilisation* /17
   ❖ Black Men in History /37

4   Booker T. Washington   51
   ❖ What I Have Learned from Black Men /51
   ❖ Address from the Dedication of the Memorial
      to Robert Gould Shaw and the Massachusetts
      54th Regiment /75

5   Carter G. Woodson   79
   ❖ Arming Black Soldiers during the U.S. Civil
      War /79
   ❖ Palmares /84

6   J. A. Rogers   87
   ❖ The Thrilling Story of the Maroons /87

7   **W. E. B. Du Bois**   93
    ❖ From *The Gift of Black Folk*
        o Chapter III – Black Soldiers /93
        o Chapter IV – The Emancipation of
           Democracy /126

8   **Elizabeth Ross Haynes**   157
    ❖ Harriet Tubman /157
    ❖ Toussaint L'Ouverture /164
    ❖ Crispus Attucks /168

    Afterword: Palmares, Quilombos, Ego-   171
    History, and Legacies by Flavio Gomes

    Who's Who of Contributors   177

    Illustrations   181

    Bibliography & Further Reading   185

FOREWORD: THE NEGRO DIGS UP HIS PAST[1]

The American Negro must remake his past in order to make his future. Though it is orthodox to think of America as the one country where it is unnecessary to have a past, what is a luxury for the nation as a whole becomes a prime social necessity for the Negro. For him, a group tradition must supply compensation for persecution, and pride of race the antidote for prejudice. History must restore what slavery took away, for it is the social damage of slavery that the present

---

[1] Originally published in 1925 in *The New Negro: An Interpretation,* edited by Alain Locke. I have maintained the use of Negro (capitalised and lower case) in this book, because it was used with pride by Black people themselves in the early twentieth century. The capital "N" was the result of a campaign led by Booker T. Washington, among others. I have also maintained the full spelling of the "n-word" found in the original essays. Note that when the authors use it, it is always in inverted commas (quotation marks) and reflects the discourse of White supremacists –Ed.

generations must repair and offset. So among the rising democratic millions we find the Negro thinking more collectively, more retrospectively than the rest, and apt out of the very pressure of the present to become the most enthusiastic antiquarian of them all.

Vindicating evidences of individual achievement have as a matter of fact been gathered and treasured for over a century: Abbé Gregoire's liberal-minded book on Negro notables in 1808[2] was the pioneer effort; it has been followed at intervals by less known and often less discriminating compendiums of exceptional men and women of African stock. But this sort of thing was on the whole pathetically over-corrective, ridiculously over-laudatory; it was apologetics turned into biography. A true historical sense develops slowly and with difficulty under such circumstances. But today, even if for the ultimate purpose of group justification, history has become less a matter of argument and more a matter of record. There is the definite desire and determination to have a history, well documented, widely known at least within race circles, and administered as a stimulating and inspiring tradition for the coming generations.

Gradually as the study of the Negro's past has come out of the vagaries of rhetoric and propaganda and become systematic and scientific, three outstanding conclusions have been established:

First, that the Negro has been throughout the centuries of controversy an active collaborator, and often a pioneer, in the struggle for his own freedom and advancement. This is true to a degree which makes it the more surprising that it has not been recognized earlier.

Second, that by virtue of their being regarded as something "exceptional," even by friends and well-wishers, Negroes of attainment and genius have been unfairly disassociated from the group, and group credit lost accordingly.

---

[2] *De La littérature des nègres ou Recherches sur leurs facultés intellectuelles, leurs qualités morales et leur littérature; suivies de Notices sur la vie et les ouvrages des Nègres qui se sont distingués dans les Sciences, les Lettres et les Arts,* by Henri Grégoire. Paris: Chez Maradan, Libraire, 1808 –Ed.

THE NEED FOR HEROES

Third, that the remote racial origins of the Negro, far from being what the race and the world have been given to understand, offer a record of credible group achievement when scientifically viewed, and more important still, that they are of vital general interest because of their bearing upon the beginnings and early development of human culture.

With such crucial truths to document and establish, an ounce of fact is worth a pound of controversy. So the Negro historian to-day digs under the spot where his predecessor stood and argued. Not long ago, the Public Library of Harlem housed a special exhibition of books, pamphlets, prints and old engravings, that simply said, to sceptic and believer alike, to scholar and school-child, to proud black and astonished white, "Here is the evidence." Assembled from the rapidly growing collections of the leading Negro book-collectors and research societies, there were in these cases, materials not only for the first true writing of Negro history, but for the rewriting of many important paragraphs of our common American history. Slow though it be, historical truth is no exception to the proverb.

Here among the rarities of early Negro Americana was Jupiter Hammon's *Address to the Negroes of the State of New York*, edition of 1787, with the first American Negro poet's famous "If we should ever get to Heaven, we shall find nobody to reproach us for being black, or for being slaves." Here was Phyllis [sic] Wheatley's Mss. poem of 1767 addressed to the students of Harvard, her spirited encomiums upon George Washington and the Revolutionary Cause, and John Marrant's St. John's Day eulogy to the "Brothers of African Lodge No. 459" delivered at Boston in 1789. Here too were Lemuel Haynes' Vermont commentaries on the American Revolution and his learned sermons to his white congregation in Rutland, Vermont, and the sermons of the year 1808 by the Rev. Absalom Jones of St. Thomas Church, Philadelphia, and Peter Williams of St. Philip's, New York, pioneer Episcopal rectors who spoke out in daring and influential ways on the Abolition of the Slave Trade. Such things and many others are more than mere items of curiosity: they educate any receptive mind.

Reinforcing these were still rarer items of Africana and foreign Negro interest, the volumes of Juan Latino, the best Latinist of Spain in the reign of Philip V, incumbent of the chair of Poetry at the University of Granada, and author of *Poems* printed there in 1573 and a book on the Escurial [*sic*] published 1576; the Latin and Dutch treatises of Jacobus Eliza Capitein, a native of West Coast Africa and graduate of the University of Leyden, Gustavus Vassa's celebrated autobiography that supplied so much of the evidence in 1796 for Granville Sharpe's attack on slavery in the British colonies, Julien Raymond's Paris exposé of the disabilities of the free people of colour in the then (1791) French colony of Hayti, and Baron de Vastey's *Cry of the Fatherland,* the famous polemic by the secretary of Christophe that precipitated the Haytian struggle for independence. The cumulative effect of such evidences of scholarship and moral prowess is too weighty to be dismissed as exceptional.

But weightier surely than any evidence of individual talent and scholarship could ever be, is the evidence of important collaboration and significant pioneer initiative in social service and reform, in the efforts toward race emancipation, colonization and race betterment. From neglected and rust-spotted pages comes testimony to the black men and women who stood shoulder to shoulder in courage and zeal, and often on a parity of intelligence and talent, with their notable white benefactors. There was the already cited work of Vassa that aided so materially the efforts of Granville Sharpe, the record of Paul Cuffee, the Negro colonization pioneer, associated so importantly with the establishment of Sierra Leone as a British colony for the occupancy of free people of colour in West Africa; the dramatic and history-making exposé of John Baptist Phillips, African graduate of Edinburgh, who compelled through Lord Bathhurst [*sic*] in 1824 the enforcement of the articles of capitulation guaranteeing freedom to the blacks of Trinidad. There is the record of the pioneer colonization project of Rev. Daniel Coker in conducting a voyage of ninety expatriates to West Africa in 1820, of the missionary efforts of Samuel Crowther in Sierra Leone, first Anglican bishop of his diocese, and that of the work of

THE NEED FOR HEROES

John Russwurm, a leader in the work and foundation of the American Colonization Society.

When we consider the facts, certain chapters of American history will have to be reopened. Just as black men were influential factors in the campaign against the slave trade, so they were among the earliest instigators of the abolition movement. Indeed there was a dangerous calm between the agitation for the suppression of the slave trade and the beginning of the campaign for emancipation. During that interval coloured men were very influential in arousing the attention of public men who in turn aroused the conscience of the country. Continuously between 1808 and 1845, men [like] Prince Saunders, Peter Williams, Absalom Jones, Nathaniel Paul, and Bishops Varick and Richard Allen, the founders of the two wings of African Methodism, spoke out with force and initiative, and men like Denmark Vesey (1822), David Walker (1828), and Nat Turner (1831) advocated and organized schemes for direct action. This culminated in the generally ignored but important conventions of Free People of Colour in New York, Philadelphia and other centres, whose platforms and efforts are to the Negro of as great significance as the nationally cherished memories of Faneuil and Independence Halls. Then with Abolition comes the better documented and more recognized collaboration of Samuel R. Ward, William Wells Brown, Henry Highland Garnett, Martin Delaney, Harriet Tubman, Sojourner Truth, and Frederick Douglass with their great colleagues, Tappan, Phillips, Sumner, Mott, Stowe, and Garrison.

But even this latter group who came within the limelight of national and international notice, and thus into open comparison with the best minds of their generation, the public too often regards as a group of inspired illiterates, eloquent echoes of their Abolitionist sponsors. For a true estimate of their ability and scholarship, however, one must go with the antiquarian to the files of the *Anglo-African Magazine*, where page by page comparisons may be made. Their writings show Douglass, McCune Smith, Wells Brown, Delaney, Wilmot Blyden, and Alexander Crummell to have been as scholarly and versatile as any of the noted publicists with whom they were associated. All of them laboured internationally in the cause of their fellows; to Scotland, England, France, Germany and Africa, they carried their brilliant offensive of debate and propaganda, and with this came instance upon instance of signal foreign recognition, from academic, scientific, public and official sources. Delaney's *Principia of Ethnology* won public reception from learned societies, Pennington's discourses an honorary doctorate from Heidelberg, Wells Brown's three year mission the entrée of the salons of London and Paris, and the tours of Frederick Douglass, receptions second only to Henry Ward Beecher's.

After this great era of public interest and discussion, it was Alexander Crummell, who, with the reaction already setting in, first organized Negro brains defensively through the founding of the American Negro Academy in 1897 at Washington. A New York boy whose zeal for education had suffered a rude shock when refused admission to the Episcopal Seminary by Bishop Onderdonk, he had been befriended by John Jay and sent to Cambridge University, England, for his education and ordination. On his return, he was beset with the idea of promoting race scholarship, and the Academy was the final result. It has continued ever since to be one of the bulwarks of our intellectual life, though unfortunately its members have had to spend too much of their energy and effort answering detractors and disproving popular fallacies. Only gradually have the men of this group been able to work toward pure scholarship. Taking a slightly different start, The Negro Society for Historical Research was later organized in New York, and has succeeded in stimulating the collection from all parts of the world of books and documents dealing with the Negro. It has also brought together for the first time co-operatively in a single society African, West Indian and Afro-American scholars. Direct offshoots of this same effort are the extensive private collections of Henry P. Slaughter of Washington, the Rev. Charles D. Martin of Harlem, of Arthur Schomburg of Brooklyn, and of the late John E. Bruce, who was the enthusiastic and far-seeing pioneer of this movement. Finally and more recently, the Association for the Study of Negro Life and History has extended these efforts into a scientific research project of great

THE NEED FOR HEROES

achievement and promise. Under the direction of Dr Carter G. Woodson, it has continuously maintained for nine years the publication of the learned quarterly, *The Journal of Negro History*, and with the assistance and recognition of two large educational foundations has maintained research and published valuable monographs in Negro history. Almost keeping pace with the work of scholarship has been the effort to popularize the results, and to place before Negro youth in the schools the true story of race vicissitude, struggle and accomplishment. So that quite largely now the ambition of Negro youth can be nourished on its own milk.

Such work is a far cry from the puerile controversy and petty braggadocio with which the effort for race history first started. But a general as well as a racial lesson has been learned. We seem lately to have come at last to realize what the truly scientific attitude requires, and to see that the race issue has been a plague on both our historical houses, and that history cannot be properly written with either bias or counter-bias. The blatant Caucasian racialist with his theories and assumptions of race superiority and dominance has in turn bred his Ethiopian counterpart—the rash and rabid amateur who has glibly tried to prove half of the world's geniuses to have been Negroes and to trace the pedigree of nineteenth-century Americans from the Queen of Sheba. But fortunately today there is on both sides of a really common cause less of the sand of controversy and more of the dust of digging.

Of course, a racial motive remains—legitimately compatible with scientific method and aim. The work our race students now regard as important, they undertake very naturally to overcome in part certain handicaps of disparagement and omission too well-known to particularize. But they do so not merely that we may not wrongfully be deprived of the spiritual nourishment of our cultural past but also that the full story of human collaboration and interdependence may be told and realized. Especially is this likely to be the effect of the latest and most fascinating of all of the attempts to open up the closed Negro past, namely the important study of African cultural origins and sources. The bigotry of civilization which is the taproot of intellectual prejudice begins far back and must be corrected at its source. Fundamentally it has come about from that depreciation of Africa which has sprung up from ignorance of her true role and position in human history and the early development of culture. The Negro has been a man without a history because he has been considered a man without a worthy culture. But a new notion of the cultural attainment and potentialities of the African stocks has recently come about, partly through the corrective influence of the more scientific study of African institutions and early cultural history, partly through growing appreciation of the skill and beauty and in many cases the historical priority of the African native crafts, and finally through the signal recognition which first in France and Germany, but now very generally, the astonishing art of the African sculptures has received. Into these fascinating new vistas, with limited horizons lifting in all directions, the mind of the Negro has leapt forward faster than the slow clearings of scholarship will yet safely permit. But there is no doubt that here is a field full of the most intriguing and inspiring possibilities. Already the Negro sees himself against a reclaimed background, in a perspective that will give pride and self-respect ample scope, and make history yield for him the same values that the treasured past of any people affords.

Arthur A. Schomburg (1874-1938)

EDITOR'S INTRODUCTION

Why did Black intellectuals feel the need for heroes? When, in a novel by Jessie Redmon Fauset, a young enslaved Black man learns about heroic figures like Frederick Douglass and Toussaint L'Ouverture, it makes him feel that if he could only escape his bondage, he could "write his name in glory."[1] In the essay that inspired the title of this anthology, published in *The Crisis* in 1941, Langston Hughes declared that there was "abundant hero material": "Do not say there are no living Negro heroes. Do not say there have never been any in the past. Those statements would be lies, enormously untrue."[2]

These individuals were role models for people who had long been told by school and history books that they were lazy, cowardly, stupid, inferior to Whites, and destined to a subservient existence—when they were not erased altogether. They were also told that enslaved Africans and their descendants were well treated and happy in captivity, and to this day, some White supremacists claim that slavery was a good thing, because it gave the captives food and shelter, and enabled them to learn useful skills. However, the story of a hero like Harriet Tubman, as told by Elizabeth Ross Haynes, will soon disabuse the reader about the "kindness" of enslavers and the supposed passivity of enslaved people or their acceptance of bondage.

Why did Black intellectuals feel the need to dig up their past? Perhaps because the German philosopher Georg Wilhelm Friedrich Hegel and, more recently, the British historian Hugh Trevor-Roper infamously declared that Africa had no history.[3] The Afro-Puerto Rican scholar Arthur (originally Arturo) Schomburg passionately disagreed, and set out to excavate Black history through his vast bibliographic collection and travels. The subtitle of this anthology was borrowed from

---

[1] Fauset, *There is Confusion*, p. 7.
[2] Hughes, "The Need for Heroes," p. 184.
[3] See Zeinab Badawi, *An African History of Africa*, pp. 243-245.

the title of the essay by Schomburg that is also the foreword. Like the other intellectuals whose works are collected in this book, he was determined to reverse the process of erasing Black people from the history books—particularly men and women of African descent whose feats, intellectual and physical, belied the negative stereotypes developed and spread by the racist ideology devised to justify their enslavement over the centuries.

One of the White supremacist authors who had the greatest influence in spreading that ideology in the United States and Brazil was a French aristocrat, Joseph Arthur Compte de Gobineau (1816-1882). Better known as Count de Gobineau, he had a major impact on intellectuals in both countries and beyond. His theories directly targeted Brazilians, because he addressed the situation of racial mixture in their country in his writings. Gobineau was a close friend of Emperor Pedro (Peter) II, whom he considered to be the only Brazilian who did not suffer from the "taint" of miscegenation.[4] Ironically, J. A. Rogers includes the Emperor, along with his father, Pedro I, and grandfather, João (John) VI, in his book *World's Great Men of Color*. According to Rogers, invoking the "one-drop rule" in a footnote to his biographical entry on Pedro II, who abolished slavery in Brazil the year before he was deposed and exiled to Portugal by a military coup in 1889:

> The Negro strain in Dom Pedro might have been about a sixteenth or less. In any case, there are Americans with less than his who are now called Negroes in America and treated as such. Pedro inherited his Negro strain more recently from his grandfather.... His family, the Braganza, had a Negro strain at least as far back as John I, the Great (1385-1422).[5]

---

[4] Gobineau and the emperor corresponded for 11 years, between 1870 and 1882. Pedro II disagreed with Gobineau, at least, in principle. In one letter, he declared that racial prejudice did not exist in Brazil: "Here, democracy means the absence of any prejudice regarding origins, faith or colour" (in Ianni, 1970, p. 268).
[5] Rogers, *World's Great Men of Color,* vol. II, "Dom Pedro II, 'The Magnanimous,' Brazilian Emancipator," References.

Count de Gobineau's influence was most widely spread by his best-known work, *Essai sur l'inégalité des races humaines* (Essay on the Inequality of the Human Races), whose title and contents led the Black Haitian intellectual Anténor Firmin to rebut it with his own work, *De l'égalité des races humaines (The Equality of the Human Races)*.

Patriotism and courage were not the only attributes which Gobineau and his followers denied to Black people. Their very existence was considered a threat to the Aryans' "purity of blood." Racial mixture arguably began in Brazil when the Portuguese explorer Pedro Álvares Cabral and his men first set foot on what they thought was the Island of Vera Cruz in 1500 and encountered the Indigenous people there. If the "one-drop rule" were applied in that country today, the vast majority of its population would be considered Black—including at least two former presidents.[6] Despite Gobineau's extreme pessimism about the outcome of miscegenation, he encouraged White Europeans to emigrate to Brazil and turn the population at least a lighter shade of tan. As a result, he predicted, "The race will be restored, public health will improve, the moral temperament will be renewed, and the happiest changes will be introduced in the social state of this admirable country."[7]

In the United States, the Count's influence took a different course. He never set foot in that country, but criticized its "decadence" in general, and enslavers in particular. Although proponents of slavery used a translation of his *Essai* to bolster their positions, Gobineau disapproved. He did not see his book as recommending the "peculiar institution." Even so, it was translated into English by Henry Hotze, a Swiss-American propagandist for the Confederacy during the U.S. Civil War, at the behest of his client, Josiah Nott, an enslaver who was looking for arguments against abolitionism.

Gobineau's followers also came up with other racialist theories, including Gustave Le Bon and Georges Vacher de Lapouge. Like

---

[6] While President of Brazil, Fernando Henrique Cardoso once commented that he had "a foot in the kitchen"—a reference to his African DNA.
[7] Gobineau, *Essai*, p. 369.

Morton, Le Bon ranked the human races according to their level of superiority, with Whites at the top. Le Bon also believed that each race had its own "soul" and ended up developing a different psychology or character—essentialist ideas that influenced American leaders such as Henry Cabot Lodge and Theodore Roosevelt.[8] Lapouge's theories were seen as extreme Gobinism combined with Social Darwinist theories of natural selection and evolution. For Lapouge, there were two human "races" in Europe: the Aryan conquerors (homo europaeus) and the conquered and enslaved, whom he called "Celts" or "Alpines" *(homo alpinus)*. Lapouge posited that these two "races" were physically and morally distinct, and that the Aryans were always preordained to dominate the others, wherever they might be found.[9] The founder of Anthroposociology, Lapouge believed that racial mixture was detrimental, and the solution was to eliminate the "inferior races" once and for all.[10]

Gobineau and Le Bon agreed that miscegenation would lead to the decline of humanity, but Lapouge opined that, much worse, it was a factor that was harmful to the "superior race": because Aryans were supposedly courageous and warlike, they would have a higher mortality rate because they fought and died in wars; they were more intensely religious, which might make them prefer celibacy, reducing their birth rate. Lapouge advocated that the most efficient way of exterminating "inferior" peoples was to encourage their vices, as they were supposedly inclined to lustfulness and drunkenness. Since Gobineau and Lapouge saw Africans as the most decadent race, this seemed to be the perfect solution to the "Black problem." Both Frenchmen maintained that, by selecting human beings deemed the fittest to procreate due to their physical and moral characteristics, eugenics would have a victorious outcome for the "Aryan race."[11]

---

[8] Dyer, *Theodore Roosevelt and the Idea of Race*, p. 10.
[9] Meréje *O problema da raça*, pp. 18-19.
[10] Pressman, "How Evolution Was Used to Support Scientific Racism."
[11] Meréje, *O problema da raça*, pp. 20-21, 24.

This is the sort of pseudoscientific thinking which Black intellectuals had to confront. Now let us take a look at some of the ways they pushed back.

BLACK VINDICATIONISM

As Arthur Schomburg observed, "Vindicating evidences of individual achievement have ...been gathered and treasured for over a century."[12] For example, in Manuel Querino's groundbreaking essay, *O colono preto como fator da civilização brasileira (The African Contribution to Brazilian Civilisation)*, we find references that are still relevant to the study of Africans and people of African descent in Brazil, including the history of the maroon communities known as *quilombos* and the most famous of them all, Quilombo dos Palmares.

According to the historian E. Bradford Burns, the author of a bibliographical essay on Querino that included his free translation of the final pages of Querino's work:

> The essay abounded with insights, many of which later scholarship adopted and expanded—so much so that it is now difficult to appreciate the originality of Querino when he first suggested them. Subsequent scholars have emphasized, for example, that Africa provided the skilled and unskilled labour which developed Brazil. However, the essay suggested other significant contributions of the Blacks on which historians have yet to dwell.[13]

For example, Burns mentions that "Querino assigned the Black a principal role in the defence of Brazil and the maintenance of national unity."[14] In *O colono preto* and other works, Manuel Querino stressed that, rather than being merely a passive source of labour, Black people had contributed significantly to the defence of Brazil and the preservation of

---

[12] Schomburg, "The Negro Digs Up His Past," p. 214.
[13] In Gledhill, ed. *Manuel Querino (1851-1923)*, pp. 8-9.
[14] Ibid., p. 9.

its national integrity. During his time in the army—and he remained in the reserves—he was in an ideal position to record the contributions of Black men, including capoeira fighters, Zuavos Baianos,[15] and volunteers who fought in the Triple Alliance War against Paraguay (1864-1870). The emphasis of this contribution to Brazilian history by Africans and their descendants is part of the tradition of Black vindicationism and had precedents in the United States. A Black American Civil War veteran, George Washington Williams stressed the contributions of Black people in his book *History of the Negro Race in America from 1619 to 1880*, a two volume work including, *Negroes as Slaves, as Soldiers, and as Citizens*, published in 1882, followed in 1887 by *A History of the Negro Troops in the War of Rebellion, 1861-1865 (The North's Civil War)*.

For Black people who were formerly enslaved or born free, the battlefront offered them a chance to prove not only their worth as upstanding citizens but their courage—giving the lie to racist stereotypes spread by the likes of Gobineau and Lapouge. One thousand Black soldiers, including two sons of the self-emancipated abolitionist, writer, and statesman Frederick Douglass, enlisted in the 54th Regiment of the State of Massachusetts. They were led by a White officer, Colonel Robert Gould Shaw, who died alongside his men and was buried with them in a common grave.[16] The courage of that first Black regiment led President Lincoln to order the recruitment of another 180,000 Black American

---

[15] Companies of Black soldiers modelled on the Zouaves, the fearsome French forces who fought against the Algerians in North Africa and wore Arab jackets, waistcoats, sashes, baggy trousers and fezzes. Martin Delany proposed creating a corps of Black Zouaves in the United States during the U.S. Civil War. White Zouave units fought on both sides during that conflict. https://www.aramcoworld.com/Articles/March-2017/America-s-Zouaves

[16] The history of this regiment entered popular culture through the film *Glory* (1989), starring Matthew Broderick, Morgan Freeman and Denzel Washington. Frederick Douglass only appears in two scenes in the film, portrayed by the actor Raymond St. Jacques, and the story omits his sons' enlistment. The film is considered a pioneer in the positive portrayal of Black history in U.S. films.

soldiers to fight in the U.S. Civil War.[17] That massive influx of Black recruits guaranteed the victory of the North, and as a result, the emancipation of enslaved people in the South.[18] Booker T. Washington recalled the exploits of the 54th Regiment in one of the most important speeches of his career, given in 1897 on the occasion of the unveiling of the monument by the Irish-born sculptor Augustus Saint-Gaudens that portrays Col. Shaw and his soldiers in bas relief. The original still stands on Boston Common, and a bronze-coloured plaster replica is one of the key exhibits in the National Gallery of Art in Washington, DC (see Frontispiece and Figs. 3 and 4).[19]

Black vindicationists also stressed another example of courage by writing about maroon communities. They were not only viewed as heroic but living proof that, far from being "happy in captivity," enslaved Africans and their descendants were determined to self-emancipate. As we will see, Black American authors also wrote about Palmares. That community still has powerful symbolic meaning in Brazil. November 20, the date on which its most famous leader, Zumbi, was killed in 1695, is now celebrated as Black Consciousness Day. A statue of Zumbi as a proud warrior stands in the Historic District of Salvador, Brazil's most African city, both historically and demographically (see Fig. 1 on p. xvii). Many view the monument as an ancestral shrine, and it frequently receives offerings of flowers.

The idea for this anthology began with a translation of Querino's work on the Black contribution to Brazil and his biographies and biographical sketches of famous Black Brazilians. Recalling Henry Louis Gates, Jr.'s comparison of Querino with Booker T. Washington,

---

[17] Massachusetts National Guard. 54 Massachusetts Volunteer Regiment. Selected Honor Guard. https://www.massnationalguard.org/index.php/history/54th-regiment.html.

[18] Hubbell, "Abraham Lincoln and the Recruitment of Black Soldiers."

[19] The French journalist known as Th. Bentzon witnessed that speech and later wrote a lengthy review of Up from Slavery. Originally published in France, it was translated into Portuguese and serialised in a Brazilian newspaper, Diário da Bahia, in 1902.

W. E. B. Du Bois, and Carter G. Woodson,[20] I began exploring their works to see if anything they wrote might compare with the translations in question. It did not take long to find that they, too, had written about the Black contribution to the U.S. in general, and highlighted the courage of soldiers and maroons, including the *quilombolas* of Palmares.

The more I dug, the more names came up, and this should not be considered an exhaustive compilation. I have included writings that were in the public domain at the time of publication, so the authors can speak for themselves. This is their book. I am merely a compiler, editor, and annotator. I hope the bibliography and suggested readings will take the reader even further.

Many friends and colleagues have contributed to this project with their moral support and encouragement. I would particularly like to thank Maurício Tesserolli, for giving permission to use his photograph of the iconic statue of Zumbi dos Palmares. Miriã Santos Araújo has, as ever, designed a brilliant book cover. I would also like to thank Flavio Gomes, a leading expert on quilombos, for writing the afterword for this anthology. His account of the maroons in Brazil and "ego-history" of his scholarship and activism provide the perfect conclusion. Last, but not least, this publication would not have been possible without the input, ideas, feedback, and support of my partner, David Pett.

Sabrina Gledhill
Devon, UK
May 2024

---

[20] Gates, Jr., *Black in Latin America*, pp. 40-41.

Fig. 1. Statue of Zumbi dos Palmares in Salvador, Bahia, Brazil.
Photo by Maurício Tesserolli

1. William Cooper Nell

From *THE COLORED PATRIOTS OF THE AMERICAN REVOLUTION*[1]
Crispus Attucks

On the 5th of March, 1851, the following petition was presented to the Massachusetts Legislature, asking an appropriation of $1,500, for the erection of a monument to the memory of CRISPUS ATTUCKS, the first martyr in the Boston Massacre of March 5th, 1770:

---

[1] From Chapter 1: Massachusetts, pp. 13-18.

1. William Cooper Nell

To the Honorable the Senate and House of Representatives of the State of Massachusetts, in General Court assembled:

The undersigned, citizens of Boston, respectfully ask that an appropriation of fifteen hundred dollars may be made by your Honourable Body, for a monument to be erected to the memory of CRISPUS ATTUCKS, the first martyr of the American Revolution.

WILLIAM C. NELL,
CHARLES LENOX REMOND,
HENRY WEEDEN,
LEWIS HAYDEN,
FREDERICK G. BARBADOES,
JOSHUA B. SMITH,
LEMUEL BURR.

BOSTON, Feb. 22d, 1851

This petition was referred to the Committee on Military Affairs, who granted a hearing to the petitioners, in whose behalf appeared Wendell Phillips, Esq., and William C. Nell, but finally submitted an adverse report, on the ground that a boy, Christopher Snyder, was previously killed. Admitting this fact, (which was the result of a very different scene from that in which Attucks fell), it does not offset the claims of Attucks, and those who made the 5th of March famous in our annals the day which history selects as the dawn of the American Revolution.

Botta's History, and Hewes's Reminiscences (the tea party survivor), establish the fact that the coloured man, ATTUCKS, was of and with the people, and was never regarded otherwise

Botta, in speaking of the scenes of the 5th of March, says:—"The people were greatly exasperated. The multitude ran towards King street, crying, 'Let us drive out these ribalds; they have no business here!' The rioters rushed furiously towards the Custom House; they approached the sentinel, crying, 'Kill him, kill him!' They assaulted him with snowballs, pieces of ice, and whatever they could lay their hands upon. The guard were then called, and, in marching to the Custom House, they

2

encountered, continues Botta, "a band of the populace, led by a mulatto named ATTUCKS, who brandished their clubs, and pelted them with snowballs. The maledictions, the imprecations, the execrations of the multitude, were horrible. In the midst of a torrent of invective from every quarter, the military were challenged to fire. The populace advanced to the points of their bayonets. The soldiers appeared like statues; the cries, the howlings, the menaces, the violent din of bells still sounding the alarm, increased the confusion and the horrors of these moments; at length, the mulatto and twelve of his companions, pressing forward, environed the soldiers, and striking their muskets with their clubs, cried to the multitude: 'Be not afraid; they dare not fire: why do you hesitate, why do you not kill them, why not crush them at once?' The mulatto lifted his arm against Capt. Preston, and having turned one of the muskets, he seized the bayonet with his left hand, as if he intended to execute his threat. At this moment, confused cries were heard: 'The wretches dare not fire!' Firing succeeds. ATTUCKS is slain. The other discharges follow. Three were killed, five severely wounded, and several others slightly."

ATTUCKS had formed the patriots in Dock Square, from whence they marched up King street, passing through the street up to the main guard, in order to make the attack.

ATTUCKS was killed by Montgomery, one of Capt. Preston's soldiers. He had been foremost in resisting, and was first slain. As proof of a front engagement, he received two balls, one in each breast.

John Adams, counsel for the soldiers, admitted that Attucks appeared to have undertaken to be the hero of the night, and to lead the people. He and Caldwell, not being residents of Boston, were both buried from Faneuil Hall. The citizens generally participated in the solemnities.

The Boston Transcript of March 7, 1851, published an anonymous communication, disparaging the whole affair; denouncing CRISPUS ATTUCKS as a very firebrand of disorder and sedition, the most conspicuous, inflammatory, and uproarious of the misguided populace, and who, if he had not fallen a martyr, would richly have deserved hanging as an incendiary.[2] If the leader, ATTUCKS, deserved the epithets above applied, is it not a legitimate inference, that the citizens who followed on are included, and hence should swing in his company on the gallows? If the leader and his patriot band were misguided, the distinguished orators who, in after days, commemorated the 5th of March, must, indeed, have been misguided, and with them, the masses who were inspired by their eloquence; for John Hancock, in 1774, invokes the injured shades of Maverick, Gray, Caldwell, ATTUCKS, Carr; and Judge Dawes, in 1775, thus alludes to the band of "misguided incendiaries":--"The provocation of that night must be numbered among the master-springs which gave the first motion to a vast machinery,--a noble and comprehensive system of national independence."

Ramsay's History of the American Revolution, Vol. I., p. 22, says— "The anniversary of the 5th of March was observed with great solemnity; eloquent orators were successively employed to preserve the remembrance of it fresh in the mind. On these occasions, the blessings of liberty, the horrors of slavery, and the danger of a standing army, were presented to the public view. These annual orations administered fuel to the fire of liberty, and kept it burning with an irresistible flame."

The 5th of March continued to be celebrated for the above reasons, until the Anniversary of the Declaration of American Independence was substituted in its place; and its orators were expected to honour the feelings and principles of the former as having given birth to the latter.

On the 5th of March, 1776, Washington repaired to the intrenchments. "Remember," said he, "it is the 5th of March, and avenge the death of your brethren!"

In judging, then, of the merits of those who launched the American Revolution, we should not take counsel from the Tories of

---

[2] The Transcript of March 5th, 1855, honourably alludes to CRISPUS ATTUCKS.

that or the present day, but rather heed the approving eulogy of Lovell, Hancock, and Warren.

Welcome, then, be every taunt that such correspondents may fling at ATTUCKS and his company, as the best evidence of their merits and their strong claim upon our gratitude! Envy and the foe do not labour to traduce any but prominent champions of a cause.

The rejection of the petition was to be expected, if we accept the axiom that a coloured man never gets justice done him in the United States, except by mistake. The petitioners only asked for justice, and that the name of CRISPUS ATTUCKS might be honoured as a grateful country honours other gallant Americans.

And yet, let it be recorded, the same session of the Legislature which had refused the ATTUCKS monument, granted one to ISAAC DAVIS, of Concord. Both were promoters of the American Revolution, but one was white, the other was black; and this is the only solution to the problem why justice was not fairly meted out.

Crispus Attucks, the First Martyr of the American Revolution, King (now State) Street, Boston, March 5th, 1770. Page 16.

2. George Washington Williams

NEGROES AS SOLDIERS
The American War of Independence[1]

As soldiers, the Negroes went far beyond the most liberal expectations of their staunchest friends. Associated with white men, many of whom were superior gentlemen, and nearly all of whom were brave and enthusiastic, the Negro soldiers of the American army became worthy of the cause they fought to sustain. Col. Alexander Hamilton had said, "*their natural facilities are as good as ours*;" and the

---

[1] Extract from Chapter XXVII of *History of the Negro Race in America from 1619 to 1880* (vol. 1), pp. 461-464.

assertion was supported by their splendid behaviour on all the battlefields of the revolution endowed by nature with a poetic element, faithful to trust, abiding in friendships, bound by the golden threads of attachment to places and persons, enthusiastic in personal endeavour, sentimental and chivalric, they made hardy and intrepid soldiers. The daring, boisterous enthusiasm with which they sprang to arms disarmed racial prejudice of its sting, and made friends of foes.

Their cheerfulness in camp, their celerity in the performance of fatigue-duty, their patient endurance of heat and cold,, and their bold efficiency in battle, made them welcome companions everywhere they went. The officers who frowned at their presence in the army at first, early learned, from experience, that they were the equals of any troops in the army for severe service in camp, and excellent fighting in the field.

The battle of Bunker Hill was one of the earliest and most important of the Revolution. Negro soldiers were in the action of the 17th of June, 1775, and nobly did their duty. Speaking of this engagement, Bancroft says, "Nor should history forget to record that, as in the army at Cambridge, so also in this gallant band, the free Negroes of the colony had their representatives."[2]

Two Negro soldiers especially distinguished themselves, and rendered the cause of the colonists great service. Major Pitcairn was a gallant officer of the British marines. He led the charge against the redoubt, crying exultingly, "The day is ours!" His sudden appearance and his commanding air at first startled the men immediately before him. They neither answered nor fired, probably not being exactly certain what was next to be done. At this critical moment, a Negro soldier stepped forward, and, aiming his musket directly at the major's bosom, blew him

---

[2] Bancroft, vol. vii, 6th ed. p. 421. [*History of the United States of America, from the Discovery of the American Continent,* by George Bancroft.. Boston: Little, Brown and co. 1874-78].

through.[3] Who was this intrepid black soldier, who at a critical moment stepped to the front, and with certain aim brought down the incarnate enemy of the colonists? What was his name, and whence came he to battle? His name was Peter Salem, a private in Col. Nixon's regiment of the Continental Army.

"He was born in Framingham [Massachusetts] and was held as a slave, probably until he joined the army: whereby, if not before, he became free…. Peter served faithfully as a soldier, during the war."[4]

Perhaps Salem was then a slave: probably he thought of the chains and stripes from whence he had come, of the liberty to be purchased in the ordeals of war, and felt it his duty to show himself worthy of his position as an American soldier. He proved that his shots were as effective as those of a white soldier, and that he was not wanting in any of the elements that go to make up the valiant soldier. Significant indeed that a Negro was the first to open the hostilities between Great Britain and the colonies, the first to pour out his blood as a precious libation on the altar of a people's rights, and that here, at Bunker Hill, when the crimson and fiery tide of battle seemed to be running hard against the small band of colonists, a Negro soldier's steady musket brought down the haughty form of the arch-rebel, and turned victory to the weak! England had loaded the African with chains, and doomed him to perpetual bondage in the North-American colonies; and when she came to forge political chains, in the flames of fratricidal war, for an English-speaking people, the Negro, whom she had grievously wronged, was first to meet her soldiers, and welcome them to a hospitable grave.

Bunker-hill Monument has a charm for loyal Americans; and the Negro, too, may gaze upon its enduring magnificence. It commemorates the deeds, not of any particular soldier, but all who stood true to the

---

[3] An Historical Research, p. 93. [An Historical Research Respecting the Opinions of the Founders of the Republic on Negroes as Slaves, as Citizens, and as Soldiers. Read before the Massachusetts Historical Society, August 14, 1862. George Livermore https://tile.loc.gov/storage-services/public/gdcmassbookdig/historicalresear00live/historicalresear00live.pdf]
[4] History of Leicester, p. 267.

principles of equal rights and free government on that memorable "17th of June."

"No name adorns the shaft; but ages hence, though our alphabets may become as obscure as those which cover the monuments, of Nineveh and Babylon, its uninscribed surface (on which monarchs might be proud to engrave their titles) will perpetuate the memory of the 17th of June. It is the monument of the day, of the event, of the battle of Bunker Hill; of all the brave men who shared its perils, alike of Prescott and Putnam and Warren, the chiefs of the day, and the coloured man, Salem, who is reported to have shot the gallant Pitcairn, as he mounted the parapet. Cold as the clods on which it rests, still as the silent heavens to which it soars, it is yet vocal, eloquent, in their undivided praise."[5]

The other Negro soldier who won for himself rare fame and distinguished consideration in the action at Bunker Hill was Salem Poor. Delighted with his noble bearing, his superior officers could not refrain from calling the attention of the civil authorities to the facts that came under their personal observation. The petition that set forth his worth as a brave soldier is still preserved in the manuscript archives of Massachusetts:

> *"To the Honourable General Court of the Massachusetts Bay.*
>
> "The subscribers beg leave to report to our Honourable House (which we do in justice to the character of so brave a man), that, under our own observation, we declare that a negro [*sic*] man called Salem Poor, of Col. Frye's regiment, Capt. Ames' company, in the late battle at Charlestown, behaved like an experienced officer, as well as an excellent soldier. To set forth particulars of his conduct would be tedious. We should only beg leave to say, in the person of this said negro centres a brave and gallant soldier. The reward due to so great and distinguished a character, we submit to the Congress.
> [signed]

---

[5] Orations and Speeches of Everett, vol. iii, p. 529.

Jona. Brewer, Col.	Eliphalet Bodwell, Sgt.
Thomas Nixon, Lt-Col.	Josiah Foster, Lieut.
Wm. Prescott, Col.	Ebenr. Varnum, 2nd Lieut.
Ephm. Corey, Lieut.	Wm. Hudson Ballart, Cpt.
Joseph Baker, Lieut.	William Smith, Cap.
Joshua Row, Lieut.	John Morton, Sergt [?]
Jonas Richardson, Capt.	Lieut. Richard Welsh

Cambridge, Dec. 5, 1775.
In Council, Dec. 21, 1775—Read, and sent down.
Perez Morton, Dep'y Sec'y[6]

How many other Negro soldiers behaved with cool and determined valour at Bunker Hill, it is not possible to know. But many were there; they did their duty as faithful men, and their achievements are the heritage of the free of all colours under our one flat. Col. Trumbull, an artist as well as a soldier, who was stationed at Roxbury, witnessed the engagement from that elevation. Inspired by the scene, when it was yet fresh in his mind, he painted the historic picture of the battle in 1786. He represents several Negroes in good view, while conspicuous in the foreground is the redoubtable Peter Salem. Som subsequent artists—mere copyists—have sought to consign this black hero to oblivion, but 'tis vain. Although the monument at Bunker Hill "does not bear his name, the pencil of the artist has portrayed the scene, the pen of the impartial historian has recorded his achievement, and the voice of the eloquent orator has resounded his valour."

---

[6] MS. Archives of Massachusetts, vol. clxxx, p. 241.

The U.S. Civil War[7]

All history, ancient and modern, Pagan and Christian, justified the conduct of the Federal Government in the employment of slaves as soldiers. Greece had tried the experiment; and at the battle of Marathon there were two regiments of heavy infantry composed of slaves. The beleaguered city of Rome offered freedom to her slaves who should volunteer as soldiers; and at the battle of Cannae a regiment of Roman slaves made Hannibal's cohorts reel before their unequalled courage. When Abraham heard of the loss of his stock, he armed his slaves, pursued the enemy, and regained his possessions. Negro officers as well as soldiers had shared the perils and glories of the campaigns of Napoleon Bonaparte; and even the royal guard at the Court of Imperial France had been mounted with black soldiers. In two wars in North America Negro soldiers had followed the fortunes of military life, and won the applause of white patriots on two continents. So then all history furnished a precedent for the guidance of the Unites States government in the Civil War in America.

But there were several aggravating questions which had to be referred to the future. In both wars in this country the Negro had fought a foreign foe an enemy representing a Christian civilization. He had a sense of security in going to battle with the colonial fathers; for their sacred battle-songs gave him purpose and courage. And, again, the Negro knew that the English soldier had never disgraced the uniform of Hampden or Wellington by practising the cruelties of uncivilised warfare upon helpless prisoners. In the Rebellion it was altogether different. Here was a war between the states of one Union. Here was a war between two sections differing in civilization. Here was a war all about the Negro; a war that was to declare him forever bond, or forever free. Now, in such a water the Negro appeared in battle against his master. For 243 years the Negro had been learning the lesson of obedience and

---

[7] Extract from Chapter XIX of *History of the Negro Race in America from 1619 to 1880* (vol. 2), pp. 261-262;274-276.

obsequious submission to the white man. The system of slavery under which he had languished had destroyed the family relation, the source of all virtue, self-respect, and moral growth. The tendency of slavery was to destroy the confidence of the slave in his ability and resources, and to disqualify him for those relations where the noblest passion of mankind is to be exercised in an intelligent matter—*amor patriae.*

Negro soldiers were required by an act of Congress to fight for the Union at a salary of $10 per month, with $3 deducted for clothing—leaving them only $7 per month as their actual pay. White soldiers received $13 per month and clothing.[8]

The Negro soldiers had to run the gauntlet of the persecuting hate of white Northern troops, and, if captured, endure the most barbarous treatment of the rebels, without a protest on the part of the Government—for at least nearly a year. Hooted at, jeered, and stoned in the streets of Northern cities as they marched to the front to fight for the Union; scoffed at and abused by white troops under the flag of a common country, there was little of a consoling or inspiring nature in the experience of Negro soldiers.

But none of these things moved the Negro soldier. His qualifications for the profession of arms were ample and admirable. To begin with, the Negro soldier was a patriot of the highest order. No race of people in the world are more thoroughly domestic, have such tender attachments to home and friends as the Negro race. And when his soul was quickened with the sublime idea of liberty for himself and kindred—that his home and country were to be rid of the triple curse of slavery—his enthusiasm was boundless. His enthusiasm was not mere animal excitement. No white soldier who marched to the music of the Union possessed a more lofty conception of the sacredness of the war for the

---

[8] This was remedied at length, after the 54th Massachusetts Infantry had refused pay for a year, unless the regiment could be treated as other regiments. Major Sturges, Agent for the State of Massachusetts, made up the difference between $7 and $13 to disabled and discharged soldiers of this regiment, until the 15th June, 1864, when the Government came to its senses respecting tis great injustice to its gallant soldiers.

Union than the Negro. The intensity of his desires, the sincerity of his prayers, and the sublimity of his faith during the long and starless night of his bondage made the Negro a poet, after a fashion. To him there was poetry in our flag—the red, white, and blue. Our national odes and airs found a response in his soul, and inspired him to the performance of heroic deeds. He was always seeing something "sublime," "glorious," "beautiful," "grand," and "wonderful" in war. There was poetry in the swinging, measured tread of companies and regiments in drill or battle; and dress parade always found the Negro soldier in the height of his glory. His love of harmonious sounds, his musical faculty, and delight of show aided him in the performance of the most difficult manoeuvres. His imitativeness gave him facility in handling his musket and sabre; and his love of domestic animals, and natural strength made him a graceful cavalryman and an efficient artilleryman.

* * *

The month of July, 1863, was memorable. Gen. Mead had driven Lee from Gettysburg, Grant had captured Vicksburg, Banks had captured Port Hudson, and Gillmore had begun his operations on Morris Island. On the 13th of July the New York Draft Riot broke out. The Democratic press had advised the people that they were to be called upon to fight the battles of the "Niggers" and "Abolitionists"; while Gov. Seymour "requested" the rioters to await the return of his adjutant-general whom he had despatched to Washington to have the President suspend the draft. The speech was either cowardly or treasonous. It meant, when read between the lines, it is unjust for the Government to draft you men; I will try and get the Government to rescind its order, and until then you are respectfully requested to suspend your violent acts against property. But the riot went on. When the troops under Gen. Wool took charge of the city, thirteen rioters were killed, eighteen wounded, and twenty-four made prisoners. The rioters rose ostensibly to resist the draft, but there were three objects before them: robbery, the destruction of the property of the rich sympathizers with the Union, and the assassination of Coloured persons wherever found. They burned the Coloured Orphans' Asylum, hung Coloured men to lamp posts, and destroyed the property of this class of citizens with impunity.

During these tragic events in New York a gallant Negro regiment was preparing to lead an assault upon the rebel Fort Wagner on Morris Island, South Carolina. On the morning of the 16th of July, 1863, the 54th Massachusetts—first Coloured regiment from the North—was compelled to fall back upon Gen. Terry from before a strong and fresh rebel force from Georgia. This was on James Island. The 54th was doing picket duty, and these early visitors thought to find Terry asleep; but instead found him awaiting their coming with all the vigilance of an old soldier. And in addition to the compliment his troops paid the enemy, the gunboats "Pawnee," "Huron," "Marblehead," "John Adams," and "Mayflower" paid their warmest respects to the intruders. They soon withdrew, having sustained a loss of 200, while Gen. Terry's loss was only about 100. It had been arranged to concentrate the Union forces on Morris Island, open a bombardment upon Fort Wagner, and then charge and take it on the 18th. The troops on James Island were put in motion to form a junction with the forces already upon Morris Island. The march of the 54th mass., began on the night of the 16th and continued until the afternoon of the 18th. Through ugly marshes, over swollen streams, and broken dykes—through darkness and rain, the regiment made its way to Morris Island where it arrived at 6 a.m. of the 18th of July. The bombardment of Wagner was to have opened at daylight of this day; but a terrific storm sweeping over land and sea prevented; It was 12:30 p.m. when the thunder of siege guns, batteries, and gunboats announced the opening of the dance of death. A semicircle of batteries, stretching across the island for a half mile, sent their messages of destruction into Wagner, while the fleet of iron vessels battered down the works of the haughty and impregnable little fort. All the afternoon one hundred great guns thundered at the gates of Wagner. Toward the evening the bombardment began to slacken until a death-like stillness ensued. To close this part of the dreadful programme Nature lifted her hoarse and threatening voice, and a severe thunder storm broke over the scene. Darkness was coming on. The brave Black regiment had reached Gen. Strong's headquarters fatigued, hungry, and damp. No time could be allowed for refreshments. Col. Shaw and Gen. Strong addressed the regiment in eloquent, inspiring language. Line of battle was formed in three brigades.... The 54th was the only regiment of Coloured men in the brigade, and to it was assigned the post of honour and danger in the front of the attacking column. The shadows of night were gathering thick and fast. Gen. Strong took his position, and the order to charge was given. On the brave Negro regiment swept amid the shot and shell of Sumter, Cumming's Point, and Wagner. Within a few minutes the troops had double-quicked a half mile; and but few had suffered from the heavy guns; but suddenly a terrific fire of small arms was opened upon the 54th. But with matchless courage the regiment dashed on over the trenches and up the side of the fort, upon the top of which Sergt. Wm. H. Carney planted the colours of the regiment. But the howitzers in the bastions raked the ditch, and hand-grenades from the parapet tore the brave men as they climbed the battle-scarred face of the fort. Here waves the flag of a Northern Negro regiment; and here its brave, beautiful, talented young colonel, Robert Gould Shaw, was saluted by death and kissed by immortality!.... One thousand and five hundred (1,500) men were thrown away in this fight, but one fact was clearly established, that Negroes could and would fight as bravely as white men....

3. Manuel R. Querino

THE AFRICAN CONTRIBUTION TO BRAZILIAN CIVILISATION[1]

[1] First published in the city of Salvador, Bahia, in 1918, "O colono preto como fator da civilização brasileira" was presented at the Sixth Brazilian Geography Conference in Belo Horizonte in 1919. Since then, it has been republished many times, generally as part of *Costumes africanos no Brasil,* a compendium of Querino's works on African and Afro-Brazilian history and culture edited by Artur Ramos and originally published in 1938 –Ed.

CHAPTER I
Portugal in the Mid-Sixteenth Century

When its audacious plans to dominate the Far East proved fruitless, Portugal turned its sights hopefully towards South America. An eminent Portuguese publicist wrote of the colonisation of Brazil: "We legislate as if the Portuguese from overseas were the pariahs of the metropolis. We govern as if Brazil were just a plantation where we brought obscure pawns and oppressed journeymen. We defend communications and the treatment of pilgrims. We have reduced a large part of its most valuable production to stagnation and monopoly.

"We forbid them to build a loom, a forge, a workshop.

"We declare it an onslaught if a single printing press timidly spreads its light in those benighted regions. We condemn literary societies as subversive.

"We fear that the slightest enlightenment of thinking will steal the emancipated colony from us."

And the same writer added:

"While we bask in the glory of daring and fortunate seafarers, we lose the reputation of energetic and far-sighted colonizers. We conquered India so that foreigners could triumph over it.

"We ravaged China, so [those foreigners] could exploit its trade.

"We took our name to Japan so that other, more fortunate ones could establish the first rudiments of Western Civilization in that singular land. We enlightened Africa so that other nations, calling us lazy and negligent, could lay claim to the land which we failed to exploit.

"Of all the endless territories we conquered, all we have left in the Far East is enough land to plant the national flag as an historical tradition."[2]

Regarding the civilising action of the Portuguese in the East, a renowned historian wrote of his countrymen:

"The Portuguese were, without a doubt, good soldiers and enterprising sailors, brave and fearless, but they were only known as conquerors. They conquered a large part of Africa and Asia, and all we know of their conquests is that so many thousand Moors or Indians allowed themselves to be beheaded with impunity by so many hundreds of Portuguese, somewhere or another.

"All we knew of the most distant regions was the riches that excited the greed of the new Argonauts; we knew nothing that could be of interest to the sciences and arts until other peoples shared equally in their spoils: it was only then that we learned about the products of Nature in those varied climes.

"Read the chronicles of those times, consult the most faithful historians, and you will see the long series of exploits alongside a pompous description of a king who was held prisoner or converted to the faith beneath an adventurer's sword. All the Portuguese left in India were ruins and tombs: much glory, if you want to count that, and nothing more."[3]

The Portuguese metropolis therefore decided to recover in Brazil what it had lost in the Levant, and here resources of all kinds could meet the needs of the moment, while ensuring a prosperous future.

In this task, however, of sailing around capes and exploring vast territories for the benefit of others, the entire fever of greatness and power of the Portuguese nation was dampened, even though its caravels

---

[2] Latino Coelho—*Elogio Histórico de José Bonifácio*—Lisbon, 1877. José Maria Latino Coelho (1825-1891) was a Portuguese general, writer, journalist, and politician –Ed.
[3] General Abreu e Lima—*Esboço Histórico, Político e Literário do Brasil.*

were involved in "cupidity, greed, hunger for gold, and thirst for conquest."[4]

Once the worst elements of the metropolis began the process of colonization, the intractable Indians revolted against the tyranny and injustice of which they were a victim, due to the exploitation of their labour in farming.

Thus began the struggles for the submission of the Indigenous peoples, wars that not even the Jesuits could stop or prevent.

Whatever the Society of Jesus achieved through persistent gentleness, with sweet and loving words, the Portuguese settlers went on to destroy through terror and force. On the one hand, affection and the desire for a fraternal and lasting alliance; on the other, punishment, torture, abuse, inconceivable torments. The orders given to Tomé de Sousa, the first governor of Brazil, determined: "Rather than negotiating peace, the governor should have some of the leaders of the uprisings arrested and order them to be hanged in their own villages."

With such colonizing methods, the poor native Americans therefore preferred to take refuge among wild animals, where freedom was the most valuable attribute of their nomadic life. Parasitism took over [the colonists] with the support of the government, which shared in the profits.

Therefore, the White settler arrived with a spirit tormented by greed, repeating the refrain of the mother country:

> "All the silver that glitters
> All the African ivory
> All the silks in China."

With devastating avarice, he threw himself into the enterprise, confident of the immediate results.

In all Spanish and Portuguese colonies, land rich in minerals fuelled the immigrant's ambitions.

---

[4] Guerra Junqueiro—*Discurso Republicano.*

The only type of man who came to the Americas was full of hopes and fears about a quick and easy fortune. No superior feeling animated him: not even the feeling of freedom.

Despotism itself was acceptable if it was reconciled with the interests of the moment.[5]

Having failed to dominate the Indigenous people who left the coast to immerse themselves in the virgin forest, Portugal changed course, and, following the example of other European nations, and, in partnership with the Arab, established its detestable dominance in the inexhaustible labour market that was the Black Continent, forcibly exporting the powerful arm of the African to the New World to boost and intensify the production of cereals and sugar cane and to extract diamonds and precious metals from the depths of the earth.

CHAPTER II
The Africans' Arrival in Brazil; Their Skills

History tells us that, long before the Christian era, the Arabs had introduced themselves into the hinterland of the Black Continent, being mainly active in the seventh century.

Muslim missionaries penetrated some parts of Africa, sowing the seeds of civilization, abolishing cannibalism and the abominable practice of human sacrifice.

Considering the level of culture achieved by these invaders, with such attributes, there is not the slightest doubt that they were the introducers of the indispensable knowledge to the African way of living in the jungles, on the plains, in the forests, in the mountains, tending flocks, and tilling fields, thus satisfying the most basic necessities of life.[6] Add to this circumstance the establishment of Portuguese trading posts

---

[5] Rocha Pombo—*História do Brasil.*
[6] Here, Querino repeats the since-refuted theory that any "civilization" found in African societies was introduced by foreign invaders –Ed.

in various parts of the Continent, and one will conclude that, when transported to the Americas, the Black colonist was already equipped for the work that awaited him here as a good hunter, sailor, livestock breeder, extractor of salt—which abounds in some regions—iron miner, shepherd, farmer, ivory merchant, etc. At the time of the slave trade, Africans were already familiar with the work of mining, as gold, silver, lead, diamonds, and iron abounded in their homeland.

And as proof that Africans had long known various material applications of the work, let us see what several explorers of the Black Continent have said in this regard:

> At Wane-Kirumbu we found a large native forge and smithy, where there were about a dozen smiths busily at work. The iron ore is very pure. Here were the broad-bladed spears of Southern Uregga, and the equally broad knives of all sizes, from the small waist-knife, an inch and a half in length, to the heavy Roman sword-like cleaver....
>
> The art of the blacksmith is of a high standard in these forests, considering the loneliness of the inhabitants. The people have much traditional lore, and it appears from the immunity which they have enjoyed in these dismal retreats that from one generation to another something has been communicated and learned, showing that even the jungle man is a progressive and an improvable animal.[7]

"They also know the processes required to manufacture steel, by combining iron and carbon and tempering."[8]

---

[7] Stanley—*Através do Continente Negro*—Vol. 2, p. 362. [*Through the Dark Continent,* vol. 2. New York: Harper & Brothers, 1878. Pp. 141-143] The Portuguese translation is slightly less patronising "A arte de ferreiro é muito apreciada nestas florestas onde, em conseqüência do seu isolamento, as aldeias são obrigadas a fazerem tudo. Cada geração aprende por sua vez os processos tradicionais, que são numerosos, e mostram que o próprio homem das solidões é um animal progressivo e perfectível" –Ed.

[8] Capello and Ivens—*De Benguela às Terras de Yacca*—Vol. 1, p. 105.

THE NEED FOR HEROES

Consultation with the gods of *feiticismo*[9] preceded the exploration of mines in Africa. Once satisfied with the affirmative response, the ritual *obligations* began, with dances, making *ebós*, and sacrificing birds and animals to ensure the success of their enterprise. Sometimes, there was also no shortage of human sacrifices.

In the midst of all their celebrations, they exclaimed: *"We must dig the earth to get rich."*

Fig. 2. Benin bronze

---

[9] This is a reference to traditional African religions. In Querino's day, they were referred to as "fetishism," but Querino preferred to use the spelling that associated it with *feitiço* (magic or sorcery). See Gledhill, "A Pioneering Afro-Brazilian Ethnologist."

Not content with enslaving the Brazilian Indian, destroying entire tribes and nations, as occurred in Maranhão and Pará, as in Guairá, in the southern zone, in the seventeenth century, and because the enslaved Indigenous people were very inconstant and less reliable, in addition to being a form of property that caused controversy between the colonists and the authorities, the colonizers of Brazil turned their covetous eyes toward Africa, and from there removed the richest merchandise that the Indigenous Americans did not provide them. The Portuguese, who left a temperate zone to settle in a fiery climate, different from that of the metropolis, could not withstand the rigours of the tropics, or fell forests and clear the land without the help of labour more accustomed to striving in these scorching regions plagued by devastating malaria.[10]

Therefore, for the Portuguese, who aimed to get rich with minimum effort, it was easy to find reason and justification for using the Black colonists acquired in Africa.

Without them, it would be difficult, if not impossible, to achieve colonization in the country solely with the European element, especially since when that process began. Aside from those occupying high administrative posts, the first waves [of European immigrants] were criminals, men of dubious repute, and common soldiers.

It was therefore necessary to import Africans from early on, and soon slave ships were depositing hundreds of Africans on the coast of Portuguese America and elsewhere, destined for farmwork and all other types of labour. Even the *bandeirante*[11] expeditions themselves did not exclude them, since whenever Black men could serve, they were pressed into service.

---

[10] Querino himself was to die of malaria in 1923 –Ed.

[11] Considered heroic figures by some—there is a major monument to the "Bandeiras" in São Paulo City—bandeirantes not only explored the interior of the continent but were often deployed to catch and enslave Indigenous people and escaped African captives, and destroy maroon settlements –Ed.

THE NEED FOR HEROES

The first gold nugget discovered on the banks of the Funil River, in Ouro Preto, was found by a Black bandeirante. A Black man also found the "Estrela do Sul" ("Star of the South") diamond. Hardworking as he was, although his body was abused by the overseer's lash, the enslaved Black always bore his lot with true stoicism.

At the end of the seventeenth century, mining began. The trafficking of Africans intensified, and many more Black colonists entered the country. Therefore, greed grew and parasitism became a social institution, with all the attendant vices and evils.

In Spanish territory, the common people who in their homeland "grunted in the darkest misery, seeking in theft and begging both entertainment and a remedy for the tortures of hunger, always deeming work beneath their dignity," also took on the arrogant airs of the upper class and nobility.

The idea of easy wealth had banished from the mind of the hungry adventurer the love of work, which was considered degrading. No matter how respectable the occupation might be, it was despised by all Portuguese with aspirations to nobility. This circumstance, however, favoured men of colour in the mechanical professions and artisan trades, as [the Portuguese] viewed apprenticeship as a punishment inflicted on the humble, as if it were an infamous occupation. Only the Blacks were set to work. "It was on Black people, imported on a prodigious scale, that the colonist especially relied to clear the vast territories conquered on the South American continent. Robust, obedient, devoted to service, the African became an invaluable collaborator of the Portuguese on the sugar mills in the North, on the plantations in the South and in the mines in the interior."

This source of labour assured, the ambitious slave-trading Portuguese felt the fever for the discovery of diamonds and gold grow. "He flaunted his wealth out of vulgar vanity, out of exaggerated ostentation, out of the vainglory of the newly rich, above all out of boredom." A contemporary witness wrote: "Women and children dress in all kinds of velvets, damasks, and other silks; and in this there is tremendous excess.

"They are mainly given to banquets, and each year they drink prodigious amounts of Portuguese wine. Banquets are served with extraordinary delicacies...and they curl up on beds of crimson damask, fringed with gold and rich bedspreads from India."[12]

There were also silver services, sedan chairs, costly horses with gold-trimmed tack, all acquired through the efforts of the heroic worker who was the obedient and industrious enslaved African; because the Portuguese had become accustomed to enjoying the fruits of labour without feeling the weight of it.

CHAPTER III
First Ideas of Freedom, Suicide, and the Violent Elimination of Enslavers

Although not generally refined in terms of wickedness and perversity, punishment on sugar mills and plantations was often harsh and sometimes cruel. Nevertheless, enslavers who committed abuses were reviled by society. When he caught an escaped captive, the slavecatcher would bind him and force him to keep pace with the horse. Sometimes two powerful enslaved men, whip in hand, would flog their fellow captive, cutting his flesh until he died in the presence of his tormenter, who witnessed that barbaric scene with satisfaction, puffed up with unbridled despotism.

In other cases, an enslaved person was put in the stocks, sometimes by the neck, suffering the tortures of hunger and thirst, with food or a jug of water deliberately placed just out of reach, while rodents bit at his feet.

In another form of punishment, the victim was bound to the back of an animal and sent far into the wilderness without food or water until he starved to death.

---

[12] Oliveira Lima—*Aspectos da Literatura Colonial Brasileira*.

THE NEED FOR HEROES

The poor wretches were overcome by nostalgia. Remembering the impetuous winds, the gentle murmur of the waterfall, the sleepy echo of the forests of his native land, tormented by the rigors of cruel slavery, and mortified by sorrows, a single idea crossed his mind, a single thought assailed his spirit: the sacred idea of freedom that was innate in his soul.

And there were those who took pity on his misfortune, dedicating these consoling verses to him:

> In my ravaged flesh,
> On my bloodstained face
> I feel the tortures from here;
> From this wretched body
> My liberated spirit
> Did not leave—it remained over there!
>
> In those hot sands,
> In that land of fire,
> Where free of chains
> I ran like the wind…
>
> There in the far reaches of the horizon...
> There on the plains...on the mountain...
> There in the heights of Heaven...
> Over the flowery forest
> This lost soul of mine
> Did not come—I alone have left.
>
> The freedom I had,
> While enslaved I did not lose it;
> My soul which lives on over there
> Turned the sombre side to me;
> The hissing of the fierce whip
> Through these shadows of the night
> Does not reach the palm trees, no,
> There I have land and flowers...
> My mother...my loves...
> Clouds and skies...my homes.[13]

---

[13] José Bonifácio the Younger. *Saudades do Escravo* (The Slave Yearns for Home).

How to win freedom?

How to obtain or regain it?

Driven by nameless despair, uncertain of obtaining that lost treasure [of freedom], without the faintest glimmer of hope, the most impetuous threw themselves into the currents of rivers or the turbulent waters of the sea under the overwhelming persuasion that they would be reborn in their beloved homeland.

"Six slaves singing, as if they did not feel the weight and degradation of the heavy forked slave-sticks in which their necks were

---

I would like to thank Sergio Guedes for his help with the interpretation and translation of this poem. Any errors are entirely my own –Ed. The original Portuguese reads:

Nas minhas carnes rasgadas,
Nas faces ensangüentadas
Sinto as torturas de cá;
Deste corpo desgraçado
Meu espírito soltado
Não partiu—ficou-me lá!

Naquelas quentes areias,
Naquela terra de fogo,
Onde livre de cadeias
Eu corria em desafogo...

Lá nos confins do horizonte...
Lá nas planícies...no monte...
Lá nas alturas do Céu...
De sobre a mata florida
Esta minha alma perdida
Não veio—só parti eu.

A liberdade que eu tive
Por escravo não perdia-a;
Minh'alma que lá só vive
Tornou-me a face sombria
O zunir do fero açoite
Por estas sombras da noite
Não chega, não, aos palmares
Lá tenho terra e flores...
Minha mãe...os meus amores...
Nuvens e céus...os meu lares

enclosed ; and, on enquiry, their words told of some idea of a future state and of a retribution—'Oh, you sent me off to Manga (sea coast), but the yoke is off when I die, and back I shall come to haunt and kill you!'"[14] Voluntary strangulation, poisonous beverages, and other tortures were the quickest means they used to end such a painful existence. Later, the enslaved people understood that the enslaver was the one who should suffer the same violent death to which the unfortunate bondspeople were subjected.

They did not hesitate for a moment, and carried out poisonings and barbaric massacres of the enslavers, overseers, and their families. Revenge raged in their souls; it was the repulsion caused by despair that the horrors of slavery inspired in them. The perversity of the treatment of the enslaved tortured even the patient, and the most extravagant reprisals came to mind.

Recognizing, however, the ineffectiveness of all this violence, the African himself retreated in horror, taking a different path.

They then resorted to collective escape and resistance, hiding in the wilderness, where they organized their own society.

CHAPTER IV
Collective Resistance, Palmares, Partial Uprisings

Amid all the sufferings that crushed the heart of the African race in Brazil, there was a moment of overwhelming relief when, deserting the sugar mills and plantations, enslaved people formed the confederation of Palmares [in the early seventeenth century] to defend their freedom.

Ancient Rome, which enslaved so many peoples, once witnessed with terror and panic a Spartacus at the head of an army of slaves.

In Brazil, too, slavery drove Africans to rise up and fight. There were slave wars with all their horrors, but in Palmares, the people gathered there had no thought of revenge: quite the contrary, their aim

---

[14] David Livingstone—*Explorações africanas.* [*Explorations in Africa*]

was to escape tyranny and live in freedom, in accordance with the noblest aspirations of man.

Greek slaves were educated both in public games and in literature, advantages that the enslaved African in the Americas was denied, as the rigors of captivity, which did not allow for the slightest mental preparation, dulled his intellect. However, he proved to be superior to the anguish of suffering, and made memorable attempts to revolt, seeking to organize a society with an independent government. He organized for war and prepared the defence of his citadel of Palmares and, when necessary, opportune incursions into neighbouring and enemy territory.

He adapted his native songs to war chants.

The Greek or Roman slave, fleeing his enslaver, did not consider organizing a regular society in any territory he happened to find; he wandered alone or in bands to pillage.

The devastation wrought by Roman slaves inspired terror in all who heard of their approach. The founders of Palmares did not act that way; they sought refuge in the vastness of virgin Nature, and there they laid the foundations of a society, imitating those that predominated in Africa, their homeland, a society, in fact, more advanced than Indigenous organizations [in the Americas]. Theirs was not a conquest driven by hatred, but a legitimate affirmation of the desire to live as free men. Thus, the Palmares refugees enacted strict laws against theft, homicide, adultery, which they rigorously observed.

Hatred against Whites did not preoccupy them; they forgave and forgot their griefs, since their entire aspiration was expressed in the joys of freedom.

In the society of Palmares, neither vagabonds nor criminals flourished; the tortured life of the slave quarters had been replaced by ready and natural comfort.

When civilized man even began to doubt whether the African or the Indian had a soul, and even the most tolerant barely granted that they did, and then only after they were baptized, the son of the black Continent gave proof that he possessed it. He revolted with indignation against the unjust oppression of which he was a victim, forcibly imposing his freedom and independence. "Of all the historical slave protests, Palmares is the most beautiful, the most heroic. It is a black Troy, and its story, an Iliad."[15]

"Palmares form the most beautiful page of African heroism and the great love of independence that the race left in the Americas."[16]

The defeat of Palmares encouraged the enslavers [to tighten] the iron yoke in which they held the enslaved; it was a reaction to the anticipation of danger. The enslaved individual from Bahia's Recôncavo,[17] in particular, was poorly fed and scantily clothed.

But the enslaved African did not rest; he held firm to the idea of regaining his lost freedom by any means possible. In 1807, Governor Count da Ponte ordered harsh measures against the quilombos, which were multiplying excessively. Just as the enslavers became even more cruel, so resentment increased and aroused a thirst for revenge among their unfortunate victims. The growing number of uprisings, some of more or less importance, in all parts, followed by massacres, are proof of this. The courage of the rebels, in the service of liberty, did not stint on sacrifice or accept unjust suffering. They had to fight, and fight heroically, given the unequal conditions.

"Once implacable hatred was ignited in the breasts of these wretched human beings, due to the barbaric punishments and mistreatment that their masters inflicted on them, it was natural that an infernal conspiracy would explode. In Bahia, on February 28, 1814, plagued by hunger and desperate due to excessive work and the habitual cruelty of the overseers, they rebelled and, taking up arms, robbed the houses and slave quarters of the plantations in Itapoã.

"The troops of the Torre Legion battled with the rebels near Santo Amaro de Ipitanga several times that same day.

---

[15] Oliveira Martins—*Portugal e as Colonias.*
[16] Rocha Pombo—*História do Brasil*—vol. 2.
[17] The area surrounding the Bay of All Saints in what is now the state of Bahia, Brazil. Well-drained by rivers and endowed with fertile soil, it was the site of numerous sugar mills and plantations –Ed.

"The Blacks fought so boldly and furiously that they only gave ground when felled by bullets."[18]

As usual, the troops tried to fight without killing to spare the masters the loss of their rebellious slaves. But the Blacks preferred to lose their lives, fighting for liberty, and fought fiercely, desperately. There was many an African Spartacus in Brazil who preferred death to captivity.

CHAPTER V
Self-Liberation Societies

Exhausted by constant struggles, restricted by all possible means in his aspirations, yet firm, resolute, and confident in his ideals, the enslaved African did not become disillusioned, he did not despair; he tried another way, in fact more in keeping with the conservative spirit of society— *trusting in his own labour.*

The unfortunate writer Afonso Arinos[19] tells us, in his excellent article "Atalaia Bandeirante," that the church of St. Iphigenia, in Alto da Cruz, in Minas [Gerais], preserves the legend of a Black king and his entire tribe, transported to that state as captives, and "levelled by the same misfortune, sovereign and vassals, the latter always kept the old faith, the same love and obedience to the king."

And the same author adds:

"At the cost of immense effort, carried out in the brief periods reserved for rest, the slave king paid for his manumission.

"Once free, he reserved the fruits of his labour to purchase the freedom of a member of his tribe; the two worked together for the third;

---

[18] Dr. Caldas Britto—*Levantes de Pretos na Bahia.*
[19] Afonso Arinos de Melo Franco (1868-1916). Querino may have described him as "unfortunate" because he died at the age of 48. His nephew of the same name was responsible for drafting the Afonso Arinos Law, which criminalised racial discrimination in Brazil –Ed.

others for the fourth, and so, successively, they freed the entire tribe. Then they built a chapel dedicated to St. Iphigenia, a Nubian princess.

"There, alongside the worship of the patron saint, they continued to venerate the Black king who was honoured by his people as a sovereign and bequeathed to the future generations what is now the legend of Chico-Rei."

Here in Bahia, the Africans did practically the same thing. Before there were savings banks (the first to be founded in Bahia dates from 1834), before emancipation funds and abolitionist societies—and before enslavers were as generous as they later became, granting letters of manumission when celebrating personal milestones—there were already special institutions for Africans to buy freedom for themselves and their descendants, funds that were called "*juntas*."

They met under the leadership of the individual who commanded the greatest respect and trust, and formed a loan society for that noble purpose. The person in charge of safeguarding the money had a unique way of recording the amounts received, amounts loaned, and interest accrued.

There was no bookkeeping at all; but, as the borrowers made their payments, the lender would indicate receipt of the agreed amounts through incisions made on a wooden stick kept for each one.

Another African was charged with collecting payments that were delivered to the leader when the debtor did not spontaneously appear.

They usually met on Sundays to receive contributions and count the amounts raised, usually in copper coin, and deal with matters related to the loans.

If the member required a given sum, he had the right to withdraw it, but the interest corresponding to the time [it was borrowed] was deducted. If the entire investment was withdrawn, the manager immediately received a certain percentage that was owed to him for holding the money deposited. Naturally, the lack of records led to difficulties for all the parties involved.

Sometimes, a member would borrow the money needed for his manumission, and, based on the manager's calculations of interest, that borrower would pay twice the amount of the loan.

At the end of each year, as with all business organizations, dividends were distributed. Heated debates arose on these occasions, although they did become violent, making police intervention unnecessary and inappropriate.

And so the captives helped each other, for the main purpose of obtaining their letters of manumission, using the funds as if they were still in the African hinterlands. Through mutual assistance and patient effort, these heroes of labour liberated themselves.

CHAPTER VI
The Africans and Their Families, Their Notable Descendants

Throughout history, letting the yellowish light of the chronicles illuminate our minds, we cannot be certain who had the greatest influence on the national formation of this land, whether the Portuguese or the Blacks. If called on to decide, our vote does not necessarily go to the former (Mello Moraes Filho).

Agriculture was the initial and enduring source of the nation's wealth.

Although it was guided by limited, routine, and superficial processes, it did not stop thriving and developing under the activity and influx of slave labour. All of the Africans' physical efforts were characterised by the idea of taking advantage of the greatest amount of agricultural production, from which the colonizers could reap an abundant harvest of profits, and it was only after the physical resistance of the enslaved people had been overcome by the rigours of work on the plantation and the heat, and above all, due to age that, in return for so much effort, they were allowed to devote themselves to different tasks in the households, that is, when death did not surprise them while labouring in the fields.

THE NEED FOR HEROES

Once transferred to the Big House, the Black slave with his affectionate nature, and, in general, good will, proven loyalty, and intelligence, albeit uneducated, won the esteem of his masters through sincere devotion and self-sacrifice. It was in the enslaver's home that Black people expanded the noblest sentiments of their soul, collaborating, with parental love, in raising the descendants of their lords and masters, cultivating obedience, deference, and respect for old age, and inspiring sympathy and even love from everyone in the family.

Black mothers were a storehouse of tenderness for the young masters, making the families of their enslavers flourish.

This conviviality in the Big House resulted in various forms of the most personal service, with the emergence of the lady's maid, the valet, the affectionate wet nurse, pages, bodyguards, and favourite servants.

These enslaved African slaves were hardworking, thrifty, and provident, qualities that their descendants did not always conserve. They sought to give their children a lawful occupation, and whenever possible, they ensured that their children and grandchildren learned a skill. It was the work of Black people that sustained the nobility and prosperity of Brazil for centuries: it was thanks to their labour that we had scientific institutions, literature, the arts, commerce, industry, and so forth, therefore making them a prominent factor in the development of Brazilian civilization.

Whoever writes Brazilian history will note the value and contribution of Black people in the defence of national territory, in farming, in mining, as an explorer, in the independence movement, bearing arms, as an important part of family life, and as the hero of labour in all its useful and profitable applications. They have been the driving force behind the nation's social, cultural, and material development, since, without the money that drives everything, there would be no teachers or students: the brightest aspirations, the most valuable attempts, would wither. It was with the fruits of their captives' labour that the wealthy enslavers sent their children to European universities, and later to the country's institutes of higher education, instructing them, educating them, resulting in venerable priests, accomplished politicians, notable scientists, excellent writers, brave soldiers, and all those who later made colonial and independent Brazil a cultured nation, powerful among civilised peoples.

From the coexistence and collaboration of the races in the creation of this country, comes this *mestiço* population of all hues, whence came this illustrious group of talented men who, in general, represented the true glory of our nation. Without any effort we can name here the Viscount of Jequitinhonha, Eunápio Deiró, the privileged Rebouças family, Gonçalves Dias, Machado de Assis, Cruz e Souza, José Agostinho, the Viscount of Inhomirim, Saldanha Marinho, Father José Maurício, Tobias Barreto, Lino Coutinho, Francisco Glicério, Natividade Saldanha, José do Patrocínio, José Teófilo de Jesus, Damião Barbosa, Chagas, *o Cabra*, João da Veiga Muricy, and many others, to speak only of the dead. This allows us to assert that Brazil possesses two real riches: the fertility of the soil and the talent of its mixed-race people.

In the case of economic wealth, the source of national organisation, the Black settler is also the leading figure, the utmost factor.

These are the flowers which adorn the brow of the persecuted and long-suffering race that will leave undying proof of its indisputable value. History in all its justice must respect and speak well of them, for the invaluable services they have provided us over the course of more than three centuries.

> As a patriot said, with good reason:
> "Whoever rereads history
> Will see the formation of
> The nation, whose only glory
> Is the African it imported."

BLACK MEN IN HISTORY[20]

DR CAETANO LOPES DE MOURA

He was eighteen years old when he found himself involved in the seditious movement of 1798.[21] At the time, he was a Latin teacher qualified to teach other subjects. To flee the investigation that was soon launched, he emigrated to foreign parts and managed to obtain a degree in Medicine from the University of Coimbra. After joining the Army Medical Corps, he fought in the Peninsular War as chief surgeon of the Portuguese Legion. Afterwards, he went to France, which afforded him more scope for his literary and scientific cogitations, settled there and, finally, became an MD. Thus equipped for greater enterprises, he devoted himself to clinical medicine and dedicated his spare time to study and scholarship. Avidly, he wrote and translated from French, English and German valuable works of history, science and literature. He served in the French Navy and was the private physician of Napoleon Bonaparte,[22] of whom he wrote a major biography. He had a great reputation as a man of letters.

---

[20] Originally published in the *Revista do Instituto Histórico e Geográfico da Bahia*, no. 48, 1923, pp. 353-363. Not all of these mini-biographies are of soldiers, but I have included the entire essay to show the range of activities and professions Querino covered—including clerics, doctors, lawyers, translators, and teachers, some of whom joined the military and/or got involved in uprisings, sometimes on opposite sides –Ed.

[21] The Bahia Conspiracy (Conjuração Baiana) or Revolt of the Tailors. Inspired by the French and Haitian revolutions, this separatist uprising took place in Bahia between 1796 and 1800. The rebels included people from various social classes, the elite and hoi polloi, civilians and soldiers, free and enslaved individuals. Although it failed and its leaders were executed, it was one of the first rebellions involving enslaved people in Brazil whose main goals included abolishing slavery –Ed.

[22] While he did serve as a surgeon in Napoleon's army, there is no evidence that he was ever Bonaparte's private physician. He was, however, a protégé of Emperor Pedro II of Brazil, who ordered and paid for his tomb to be maintained in perpetuity at the Père-Lachaise cemetery in Paris –Ed.

The illustrious Hellenist Odorico Mendes said in his regard: "Our illustrious compatriot is extremely rich linguistically." Old, ailing, and forsaken, he was supported by the munificence of Emperor Pedro II, who granted him a modest pension that enabled him to live a less troubled life. He was a native of Bahia who brought honour to his homeland, particularly abroad, where he won the admiration of the most eminent spirits of the Old World through his literary knowledge and profound scholarship. This circumstance enhanced his intellectual value even more, as he was a man of colour who came from a country that is now poorly judged by nations that call themselves proponents of progress, science, the arts, and literature.

Here is a list of works that bore his mark, original or translated:

1—*Os Incas ou a destruição do Império do Peru* (1837)[23]
2—*D. Ignez de Castro* (1837)[24]
3—*O Talismã* (1837)[25]
4—*Os Puritanos na Escócia* (1837)[26]
5—*Os Natchez* (1837)[27]
6—*Contos a meus filhos* (1838)[28]
7—*O derradeiro moicano* (1838)[29]
8—*O Piloto* (1838)[30]
9—*O Escocês na Corte de Luiz XI* (1838)[31]
10—*Arte de curar a si mesmo* (1839)[32]
11—*Máximas e sentenças morais* (1840)
12—*Waverley ou há dezoito anos* (1844)[33]

---

[23] *The Incas: Or, the Destruction of the Empire of Peru,* by M. Marmontel
[24] *Ignez de Castro, a Tragedy,* by Antonio Ferreira
[25] *The Talisman,* by Sir Walter Scott
[26] *The Puritans,* by Sir Walter Scott
[27] *The Natchez Indians: A History to 1735,* by James F. Barnett
[28] Tales for My Children
[29] *The Last of the Mohicans,* by James Fenimore Cooper
[30] *The Pilot: A Tale of the Sea,* by James Fenimore Cooper
[31] *Quentin Durward,* by Sir Walter Scott
[32] The Art of Self-Healing
[33] *Waverley,* by Sir Walter Scott

THE NEED FOR HEROES

13—História dos cães célebres (1845)[34]
14—Deus é todo puro amor (1849)[35]
15—História da guerra entre o Brasil e a Holanda de 1624 a 1625 (1844)[36]
16—Livro indispensável (coleção de receitas concernentes às artes, ofícios e economia doméstica e rural) (1845)[37]
17—Harmonias da Criação. Considerações sobre as maravilhas da natureza (1846)[38]
18—História de Napoleão Bonaparte, desde o seu nascimento até a sua morte (1846)[39]
19—Dicionário Histórico, Descritivo e Geográfico do Império do Brasil[40]
20—A Prisão de Edimburgo[41]
21—Ivanhoé ou o regresso do Cruzado[42]
22—Misantropia e arrependimento[43]
24—Arthur ou dezesseis anos depois[44]
25—Cartas de Heloísa a Abeilard[45]
26—Cancioneiro Alegre de El-rei D. Diniz[46]
27—Guia da conversação moderna (em francês e português)[47]

---

[34] A History of Famous Dogs
[35] God is All Pure Love
[36] History of the War Between Brazil and Holland from 1624 to 1625
[37] The Indispensable Book (collection of prescriptions concerning arts, crafts and domestic and rural economy), by Lopes de Moura (the original title was *O livro indispensável ou novíssima coleção de receitas concernentes às artes, ofícios e economia doméstica e rural, coligidas das obras mais célebres, recentemente publicadas em França e Inglaterra, 1845).*
[38] Harmonies of Creation. Considerations about the wonders of nature, by Lopes de Moura
[39] The Story of Napoleon Bonaparte, from His Birth until His Death, by Lopes de Moura
[40] Historical, Descriptive and Geographic Dictionary of the Empire of Brazil, by Milliet de Saint-Adolphe
[41] *The Heart of Midlothian,* by Sir Walter Scott
[42] *Ivanhoe*, by Sir Walter Scott
[43] *The Black Dwarf,* by Sir Walter Scott
[44] *Arthur, or Sixteen Years Later*, an 1839 drama by V.S. Mezhevich
45 *Letters of Heloise to Abelard*
[46] Joyous Songbook of King Diniz
[47] Modern Conversation Guide (in French and Portuguese)

28—*Autobiografia do Dr Caetano Lopes e Moura*[48]
29—*Estudo sobre o direito do Brasil sobre a Ilha da Trindade*[49]
30—*Tratado de Geografia Universal, física, política e histórica*[50]
31—*Geografia Elementar do Império do Brasil*[51]
32—*Prefácio e notas sobre Os Lusíadas de Camões*[52]
33—*Epítome Cronológico da História do Brasil, para uso da mocidade*[53]
34—*Mitologia da Mocidade*[54]
35—*Jesus cristo perante o século*[55]
36—*Mês de Maria ou a nova imitação da Santíssima Virgem*[56]

FATHER EUTÍCHIO PEREIRA DA ROCHA

Ordained as a priest, he devoted himself to teaching young people, and established a secondary school where he taught philosophy. Years later, he removed to the state of Pará, where he held the post of president of the Carmelite Convent and distinguished himself in political journalism as a bold polemicist. He wrote *Curso de filosofia racional e moral* [Course in Rational and Moral Philosophy], in two volumes; *Psicologia, sensibilidade e atividade da alma* [Psychology, Sensibility and Activity of the Soul]; *A consciência moral* [The Moral Conscience], and other works that were published in the periodical *Crepúsculo*[57] in Bahia.

---

[48] Autobiography of Dr Caetano Lopes e Moura, commissioned by Emperor Pedro II
[49] Study of Brazilian Law on the Island of Trindade (Trindade and Martim Vaz)
[50] Treatise on Universal Geology, Physics, Politics, and History
[51] Elementary Geography of the Brazilian Empire
[52] Preface and Notes on Camões's Lusiads
[53] Young People's Chronological Summary of the History of Brazil, by Lopes de Moura
[54] Young People's Mythology, by Lopes de Moura
[55] Jesus Christ before the Century
[56] The Month of Mary or the New Imitation of the Holy Virgin
[57] *Crepusculo periódico instructivo e moral do Instituto Literário da Bahia* [Twilight – Instructive and Moral Periodical of the Literary Institute of Bahia].

As Canon of Pará Cathedral and a Freemason, he engaged in a forceful debate in the press with Bishop Dom Antônio de Macedo Costa regarding the religious question.[58]

JOAQUIM MANUEL DE SANT'ANNA

A pharmacist with a degree from the School of Medicine, fluent operator, poet, citizen of elevated merit, versed in natural science and a Knight of the Order of the Rose.

He wrote a compendium entitled *Filosofia da Família* [Philosophy of the Family], which he did not publish. For a long time, he lived in the town of Cachoeira, where he ran a pharmacy and chemical laboratory, and for a few years, he held the post of secretary of the Ginásio da Bahia [secondary school]. At the time of his death, he was chief librarian of the Public Library.

EMÍLIO DE SANT'ANNA PINTO

Passed over in the competition for the post of permanent vicar in Abrantes parish, he lost to his rival, Dr Antônio de Macedo Costa, later Bishop of Pará and Archbishop of Bahia.

He was an honorary canon of the Metropolitan See.

PEDRO VIEIRA DOS SANTOS

[He was] canon and vicar of the parish of Itaparica [Bahia], Knight of the Order of Christ.

DR SYMPHRONIO OLYMPIO DOS SANTOS LIMA

At the time of his death, he was a captain/doctor in the Army Medical Corps in the Mato Grosso garrison.

---

[58]The "questão religiosa" involved a dispute between Ultramontan clerics who emphasised papal authority and Freemasons in Brazil in the 1870s. Dom Antônio de Macedo Costa, (Maragogipe, Bahia, 1830—Barbacena Minas Gerais, 1891) was a Primate Archbishop of Brazil. He was sentenced to four years of forced labour for sedition, but after eighteen months, the Crown granted him a pardon –Ed.

DR SYMPHRONIO OLYMPIO DOS SANTOS PITTA
A graduate of the School of Medicine, when he died, he was a lieutenant captain in the Navy Medical Corps.

DR JOSÉ PAULO ANTUNES
He had a medical degree [from the] School of Medicine, where his time as a distinguished student left an indelible mark. He went to live to the state of Rio Grande do Norte, where he practised clinical medicine and made his fortune in that profession. He also held the post of doctor of medicine in Porto [Portugal].

DR TIBÚRCIO SUZANO DE ARAÚJO
Student-teacher at the Normal School, pharmacist and doctor of medicine, and a highly regarded clinician. He was appointed a commander by the Holy See.

EMÍGDIO AUGUSTO DE MATTOS
An apprentice bricklayer, shortly after leaving primary school, he left that trade to become a hairdresser. One day, he solved an arithmetic problem he found in a compendium on that subject. This led to his love for the study of mathematics, which he learned from the engineer Maia Bittencourt, doing so well that [Maia Bittencourt] considered him a favourite pupil.

Following his teacher's advice, he devoted himself resolutely to teaching, from which he earned a living that enabled him to study the mathematical fields of learning required for a career in engineering.

In 1882, he went to Rio de Janeiro, where he enrolled in the Polytechnic School and obtained a distinction in the first and second years of the civil engineering programme before passing away during his third year. He tutored one of Emperor Pedro II's grandsons, his classmate, because Emígdio Mattos was not only a student but explained the lessons taught in the classroom to his classmates. The first time the student from Bahia underwent an oral examination was a triumph. During his brilliant exposition on the blackboard, he referred to a second-year subject on the question, and spoke and presented his thesis so confidently that the professor asked him who had taught him mathematics.

During the latter period of the monarchy, most primary school teachers in that city and its outskirts were Black men. Contemporaries nostalgically recall those friends of their childhood.

MANUEL FLORENCIO DO ESPÍRITO SANTO

The most respected member of the teaching profession, and one of its most brilliant minds, he wrote *Rudimentos gramaticais da língua portuguesa* [Basic Portuguese Grammar], which was very well received, as well as a compendium on the metric decimal system in *Aritmética elementar* [Elementary Arithmetic]. When he retired, provincial deputy Arthur Rios said, on behalf of his peers, that they were granting him his pension but regretted that primary education was being deprived of that eminent educator' brilliance. For a long time, however, he ran the "Colégio Florêncio" [secondary school] in the building which now houses the Ginásio Ypiranga [secondary school], in the Sodré [Mansion].

MIGUEL MOREIRA DE CARVALHO

After passing a competitive examination, he was appointed as a Latin teacher in the town of Maragogipe [Bahia]. Afterwards, when that post was eliminated, he taught proficiently at a primary school in Vitória parish [Salvador].

He participated brilliantly in educational conferences, where he discussed matters related to teaching with erudition.

MALAQUIAS PERMÍNIO LEITE

He was a laureate student of the renowned "Colégio Sete de Setembro," a secondary school directed by the scholar Luís da França Pinto de Carvalho.

Permínio Leite was a highly valued schoolmaster and an excellent draftsman, who won a prize at the 1875 Exposition.

SAMUEL FLORÊNCIO DE PASSOS

Deeply devoted to primary education, which garnered him well-earned renown, he wrote a compendium on elementary arithmetic and etymology for primary schools. He was a substitute teacher of Methodology at the Normal School.

ELIAS DE FIGUEIREDO NAZARETH

He began his career in primary education by teaching the practical class in pedagogy at the Normal School. Later promoted to teach Universal Geography and History, he finally held the post of director of that same establishment.

He published a compendium entitled *Desenho linear* (Linear Drawing), interesting notes on the former Liceu Provincial, now the Ginásio da Bahia, from 1836 to 1890, as well as an historical note on the founding of the Normal School. He was commissioned by the Ministry of the Empire to study the progress made in primary education in the republics of the River Plate. He represented the state government and the Geographic and Historical Institute of Bahia at the Geography Conference held in São Paulo, and belonged to several literary associations.

JOÃO PEREIRA DA CONCEIÇÃO

A modest author devoted to philosophical studies.

André Gomes de Brito, Maximiano Soares Lopes, Manoel Luiz Gomes Vinhas, André Avelino de Sousa, Francisco de Assis Trinchão were some of the other primary school teachers who greatly advanced the cause of teaching.

In the past, a young person's education was judged by the teacher from whom he learned to read and write.

DR PORFÍRIO VELLOSO

Graduated in Law, he lived in the district of Inhambupe [Bahia], [and] was a learned citizen with great prestige and political influence.

DR ELPÍDIO JOAQUIM BARAÚNA

While a fourth-year student, he joined the Paraguay campaign[59] as second-surgeon in the Army Medical Corps.

DR RUFINO JOSÉ MUTAMBA

He was a distinguished student since secondary school. Having become a clinical intern through a competitive examination, at Misericórdia [Mercy] Hospital, when he died he was a first-lieutenant/doctor in the Army Medical Corps.

DR LEANDRO PAULO ANTIGONO

He held a Law degree, and at the time of his death he was a magistrate in the state of Amazonas.

DR JOSÉ BONIFÁCIO DO PATROCÍNIO

He was a brilliant student at the School of Medicine, obtaining a distinction, including in his defence of his doctoral thesis.

DR ANSELMO PEREIRA LACERDA

He attended primary and secondary school at the "Colégio Florêncio." His training at the Law School in this state was awarded with distinctions. He settled in the state of Amazonas, where he was a magistrate.

JOÃO BAPTISTA HENRIQUES DE PAIVA

He distinguished himself as an expert organist in the Metropolitan Cathedral, taught piano, was well-versed in Latin, and [held the post of] functionary of the Church Secretariat.

JOÃO BISPO DA EGREJA

A distinguished piano teacher and a concert pianist of merit. He performed in several major Brazilian cities, particularly at the Lyric

---

[59] Also known as the Triple Alliance War –Ed.

Theatre in Rio de Janeiro in the presence of their imperial majesties, which led to his appointment as capellmeister at the Metropolitan See and the honours of a musician of the Imperial Chamber. Her Excellency the Countess of Barral e Pedra Branca presented him with a silver trumpet, an instrument on which he was without compare.

MANUEL ALVES

He acted as an ambassador for King João VI, and later for Emperor Pedro I as well. He played an active role in the Sabinada revolt of 1837.[60] Arrested by government troops, he was imprisoned in the Navy Arsenal galleys and died there. He was a knight of the Order of Christ.

During that same uprising, the famous [Black militia major José de] **Santa Eufrásia**[61] won great renown. Seeing that there was a reward for his arrest on condition that he be taken alive, when captured, he bravely took his own life.

MANUEL GONÇALVES DA SILVA

As a lieutenant colonel in the Henriques Legion, he commanded the 3rd Hunters Battalion, gaining prominence in the war for Independence in which, at his request, he held the most dangerous positions, always victorious. When Colonel Felisberto Gomes Caldeira was murdered in 1824, as the most senior officer in the garrison Manuel Gonçalves took command of the army and governed as president of the province until

---

[60] The Sabinada Rebellion (November 1837 to March 1838), was a separatist movement in Bahia, Brazil, that broke out during the Regency period, when Dom Pedro II was still a minor. Led by Francisco Sabino da Rocha Vieira (the physician and journalist who lent his name to the revolt) and the lawyer João Carneiro da Silva, its aims were complex and sometimes murky. It was mainly intended to establish an independent "Republic of Bahia," at least temporarily. Some of its participants advocated abolishing slavery. The rebels held Salvador for four months before the government forces brutally crushed the uprising. For more information, see Duarte and Saba, "The Sabinada Rebellion" –Ed.

[61] See Kraay "'As Terrifying as Unexpected,'" p. 519 –Ed.

the unrest subsided.[62] In 1826, Emperor Pedro I praised him for his good form on parade, with his battalion polished and well disciplined, surpassing all others in their manoeuvres. He was one of the signatories of the oath to the Political Constitution of Brazil in this city [Salvador], together with the other officials on May 3, 1824.

FRANCISCO XAVIER BIGODE

A seminarian when he left the religious life and joined the military. As a lieutenant colonel, he commanded the 92nd Hunters Battalion after rendering distinguished service in the war for Independence, as well as on the occasion of the African uprising of 1835.[63] He was killed as a rebel by Pernambuco troops in 1837 in the Palma barracks, to which he had retreated.[64]

LUIZ GONZAGA PAU-BRAZIL

In 1834, he was elected president of the City Council of [Salvador]. He played an active role in the revolt of 1837. He was a student at the Recife Law School but did not complete his degree.

FRANCISCO QUIRINO DO ESPÍRITO SANTO

A veteran of the Independence War, he organised the first company of "Zuavos Baianos" and fought in the Paraguay campaign with the post of captain.

---

[62] The Periquitos Mutiny, involving a mainly Black battalion that rebelled against the increasingly authoritarian regime of Emperor Pedro I. It took place between October and November 1824. The Periquitos (parakeets) got their name because of their colourful, green-trimmed uniforms (see Reis and Kraay, "The Tyrant Is Dead!") –Ed.

[63] Querino is referring to the "Revolt of the Malês," which was led by enslaved and freed Muslim Africans (see Reis, *Slave Rebellion in Brazil*) –Ed.

[64] This indicates that Bigode fought on the losing side of the Sabinada rebellion— see note 60 –Ed.

JOAQUIM DE SANTANNA GOMES

He held the post of captain adjutant to General Labatut during the War for Independence[65] and was an organist at the Third Order of St. Francis Church (Ordem Terceira de São Francisco).

MANUEL FERNANDES DO Ó

A retired militia captain and architect.

NICOLAU TOLENTINO CANNAMIRIM

In his time, he was a solicitor with a large clientele, a city councillor, and a captain in the rebel army in 1837 [the Sabinada rebellion].

JOSÉ SOARES CUPIM

He went to fight in the Paraguay campaign as a second cadet-sergeant in the first company of "Zuavos Baianos." While there, he acted with patriotism and valour that have never been belied by the people of Bahia, in defence of his country's honour. He was always preferred by the reconnaissance parties when the Army corps advanced.

One day, fed up with that assignment, he cried: "Could it be that I am the army's fool, who is sent to the most dangerous positions?" No, the adjutant to the Chiefs of Staff who had given him the order replied: "You are an officer of proven worth on the battlefield. That is why you have the confidence of your superiors."

He was praised many times in the order of the day for his duteous service in assaults. He obtained the rank of captain, won through his achievements, the medals of the Brazilian and Argentine Army, and the certificate of a knight of the Order of Christ.

He died after the war, after returning to his native land.

---

[65] What was then the province of Bahia fought for its independence from Portugal with the aid of a French general, Pierre (Pedro) Labatut (1776-1849). The war was won on July 2, 1823, and Bahia still celebrates that date as its independence day (Brazil's national independence day is September 7) –Ed.

MARCOLINO JOSÉ DIAS

Once the Paraguay War was declared, he was a sergeant in a National Guard battalion. He organised the second company of "Zuavos Baianos" and went to the front as a lieutenant, commanding them.

His superiors always praised him for the cool head and bravery he showed in battle. Under those conditions, he had the glory of planting the Brazilian flag when taking Fort Curuzú on 3 September 1866, crying with enthusiasm: "The Black Bahian Zuavo was here."

On that occasion, he received the rank of captain and the title of knight of the Order of the Cross, the [Brazilian] empire's highest.

FELICIANO CÂNDIDO PIMENTEL

Having left his job at the former Navy Arsenal, he enlisted in the Voluntários da Pátria battalion called Princesa Leopoldina and went to fight in the Paraguay War with the post of lieutenant. After the war, he returned to his homeland as a captain and held the following commissions in the Ministry of War: adjutant to General Deodoro da Fonseca, when he was an inspector of the first-line corps and military installations in the Province of Bahia; adjutant of the commander of Fort da Lage when the Navy mutinied in 1893,[66] and at the time of his death, he was an honorary lieutenant colonel in the Army, the manager of the Gunpowder Magazine in Bahia. A knight of the Order of the Rose, his war medals included that of Military Merit.

CONSTANTINO[67] LUIZ XAVIER BIGODE

The son of lieutenant colonel Francisco Xavier Bigode, already mentioned in this paper. Feeling love of country beating in his heart, Constantino Bigode set aside his workers' tools and marched off to the Paraguay War as a first cadet in the first company of "Zuavos Baianos." In Rio de Janeiro, he was promoted to second sergeant and went on to the front.

---

[66] A reference to the Naval Revolt in Rio de Janeiro (see Smith, *A History of Brazil*, pp. 91-92 et seq) –Ed.

[67] Constâncio in the original, although the correct name is given in the text –Ed.

3. MANUEL R. QUERINO

In the Battle of Curupaity, on September 22, 1866, Bigode—by then a cadet and sergeant adjutant in the 47th Corps of Voluntários da Pátria (Nation's Volunteers), he was thrice wounded and fell prisoner to the dictator of Paraguay, which he remained for two years and seven months, enduring indescribable tortures. When he was freed by the Brazilian Army and sent to serve in the 3rd Infantry Battalion, he held the post of assistant teacher of the carpenters at the Navy Arsenal in the town of Ibicuhy [Ybycuí, Paraguay].

He also fought in the battles of Peribebuy [Piribebuy], Campo Grande, and Reconhecimento, conducting himself so well that the commander-in-chief of the Army, the Count of Eu,[68] promoted him to second lieutenant for his bravery, and later to lieutenant, decorated with the Order of the Rose.

CEZÁRIO ÁLVARO DA COSTA

He served in the Paraguay War as a corporal in the 7th Infantry Battalion of the Army. He distinguished himself in combat on numerous occasions, reaching the rank of captain of that same battalion due to acts of courage.

In addition to war medals, he held that of Military Merit and the habit of a knight of the Imperial Order of the Cross.

FRANCISCO BARBOSA D'OLIVEIRA

He organised the third company of "Zuavos Baianos" and died in Paraguay with the rank of captain. He used to encourage his soldiers in combat, saying: "Forward, forward, victory is ours."

The following lieutenants also distinguished themselves: **Nicolau da Silveira**, knight of the Order of the Rose, **Firmino José das Dores, Bernardino de Senna Cajá, Eugênio Moniz**, and the second-lieutenants: **Emiliano José Miguel, José Quirino Catuladeira**, and **André Fernandes Galiza**.

---

[68] Gaston d'Orleans, the Count of Eu, was married to Princess Isabel, the daughter of Emperor Pedro II, and heiress to the throne who is credited with officially abolishing slavery in Brazil in 1888 –Ed.

4. Booker T. Washington

WHAT I HAVE LEARNED FROM BLACK MEN[1]

N o single question is more often asked me than this: "Has the pure blooded black man the same ability or the same worth as those of mixed blood?"[2]

It has been my good fortune to have had a wide acquaintance with black as well as brown and even white Negroes. The race to which

---

[1] Chapter IX of *My Larger Education.*

[2] Booker T. Washington's enslaved mother, Jane, was Black, and his biological father (whom Washington declined to name) was White. Even in his obituaries, some writers attributed Washington's talents to his White ancestry, something which he emphatically refutes in this essay –Ed.

I belong permits me to meet and know people of all colours and conditions. There is no race or people who have within themselves the choice of so large a variety of colours and conditions as it true of the American Negro. The Japanese, as a rule, can know intimately human nature in only one hue, namely, yellow. The white man, as a rule, does not get intimately acquainted with any other than white men. The Negro, however, has a chance to know them all, because within his own race, and among his own acquaintances, he has friends, perhaps even relatives, of every colour in which mankind has been painted.

Perhaps I can answer the question as to the relative value of the pure Negro and the mixed blood in no better way than by telling what I know concerning, and what I have learned from, some four or five men of the purest blood and the darker skins of any human beings I happen to know—men to whom I am indebted for many things, but most of all for what they have done for me in teaching me to value all men at their real worth regardless of race or colour.

Among those black men whom I have known, the one who comes first to my mind is **Charles Banks** of Mound Bayou, Miss., banker, cotton broker, planter, real estate dealer, head of a $100,000 corporation which is erecting a cotton seed oil mill, the first ever built and controlled by Negro enterprise and Negro capital, and finally, leading citizen of the little Negro town of Mound Bayou.

I first met Charles Banks in Boston. As I remember, he came in company with Hon. Isaiah T. Montgomery the founder of Mound Bayou, to represent, at the first meeting of the National Negro Business League in 1900, the first and at that time the only town in the United States founded, inhabited, and governed exclusively by Negroes. He was then, as he is today, a tall, big-bodied man, with a shiny round head, quick, snapping eyes, and a surprisingly swift and quiet way of reaching out and getting anything he happens to want. I never appreciated what a big man Banks was until I began to notice the swift and unerring way in which he reached out his long arm to pick up, perhaps a pin, or to get hold of the button hole and of the attention of an acquaintance. He seemed to be able to reach without apparent effort anything he wanted, and I soon found there was a certain fascination in watching him move.

I have been watching Banks reach for things that he wanted, and get them, ever since that time. I have been watching him do things, watching him grow, and as I have studied him more closely my admiration for this big, quiet, graceful giant has steadily increased. One thing that has always impressed itself upon me in regard to Mr. Banks is the fact that he never claims credit for doing anything that he can give credit to other people for doing. He has never made any effort to make himself prominent. He simply prefers to get a job done and, if he can use other people and give them credit for doing the work, he is happy to do so.

At the present time Charles Banks is not, by any means, the wealthiest, but I think I am safe in saying that he is the most influential, Negro business man in the United States. He is the leading negro banker in Mississippi, where there are eleven Negro banks, and he is secretary and treasurer of the largest benefit association in that state, namely, that attached to the Masonic order, which paid death claims in 1910 to the amount of $195,000 and had a cash balance of $80,000. He organized and has been the moving spirit in the state organization of the Business League in Mississippi and has been for a number of years the vice president of the National Negro Business League.

Charles Banks is, however, more than a successful business man. He is a leader of his race and a broad-minded and public-spirited citizen. Although he holds no public office, and, so far as I know, has no desire to do so, there are, in my opinion, few men, either white or black, in Mississippi today who are performing, directly or indirectly, a more important service to their state than Charles Banks.

Without referring to the influence that he has been able to exercise in other directions, I want to say a word about the work he is doing at Mound Bayou for the Negro people of the Yazoo Delta, where, in seventeen counties, the blacks represent from seventy-five to ninety-four percent of the whole population.

As I look at it, Mound Bayou is not merely a town; it is at the same time and in a very real sense of that word, a school. It is not only a place where a Negro may get inspiration, by seeing what other members of his race have accomplished, but a place, also, where he has an opportunity to learn some of the fundamental duties and responsibilities of social and civic life.

Negroes have here, for example, an opportunity, which they do not have to the same degree elsewhere, either in the North or in the south, or entering simply and naturally into all the phases and problems of community life. They are the farmers, the business men, bankers, teachers, preachers. The mayor, the constable, the aldermen, the town marshal, even the station agent, are Negroes.

Black men cleared the land, built the houses, and founded the town. Year by year, as the colony has grown in population, these pioneers have had to face, one after another, all the fundamental problems of civilization. The town is still growing, and as it grows, new and more complicated problems arise. Perhaps the most difficult problem the leaders of the community have to face now is that of founding a school, or a system of schools, in which the younger generation may be able to get some of the kind of knowledge which these pioneers gained int eh work of building up and establishing the community.

During the twenty years this town has been in existence it has always had the sympathetic support of people in neighbouring white communities. One reason for this is that the men who have been back of it were born and bred in the Delta, and they know both the land and the people.

Charles Banks was born and raised in Clarksdale, a few miles above Mound Bayou, where he and his brother were for several years engaged in business. It was his good fortune, as has been the case with many other successful Negroes, to come under the influence, when he was a child, of one of the best white families int eh city in which he was born. I have several times heard Mr. Banks tell of his early life in

Clarksdale and of the warm friends he had made among the best white people in that city.

It happened that his mother was cook for a prominent white family in Clarksdale. In this way he because in a sort of way attached to the family. It was through the influence of this family, if I remember rightly, that he was sent to Rust University, at Holly Springs, to get his education.

In 1900 Mr. Banks, because of his wide knowledge of local conditions in that part of the country, was appointed supervisor of the census for the Third district of Mississippi. In speaking to me of this matter Mr. Banks said that every white man in town endorsed his application for appointment.

Since he has been in Mound Bayou, Mr. Banks has greatly widened his business connections. The Bank of Mound Bayou now counts among its correspondents banks in Vicksburg, Memphis, and Louisville, together with the National Bank of Commerce of St. Louis and the National Reserve Bank of the city of New York. One of the officers of the former institution, Mr. Eugene Snowden, in a recent letter to me, referring to this and another Negro bank, writes: "It has been my pleasure to lend them $30,000 a year and their business has been handled to my entire satisfaction."

Some years ago, in the course of one of my educational campaigns, I visited Mound Bayou, among other places in Mississippi. Among other persons I met the sheriff of Bolivar County, in which Mound Bayou is situated. Without any suggestion or prompting on my part, he told me that Mound Bayou was one of the most orderly—in fact, I believe he said the most orderly—town in the Delta. A few years ago a newspaper man from Memphis visited the town for the purpose of writing an article about it. What he saw there set him to speculating, and among other things he said:

> Will the Negro as a race work out his own salvation along Mound Bayou lines? Who knows? These have worked out for themselves a better local government than any superior people has ever done for them in freedom. But it is a generally accepted

principle in political economy that any homogeneous people will in time do this. These people have their local government, but it is in consonance with the county, state, and national governments and international conventions, all in the hands of another race. Could they conduct as successfully a county government in addition to their local government and still under the state and national governments of another race? Enough Negroes of the Mound Bayou type, and guided as they were in the beginning, will be able to do so.

The words I have quoted will, perhaps, illustrate the sort of interest and sympathy which the Mound Bayou experiment arouses in the minds of thoughtful Southerners. Now it is characteristic of Charles Banks that, in all his talks with me, he has never once referred to the work he is doing as a solution of the problem of the Negro race. He has often referred to it, however, as one step in the solution of the problem of the Delta. He recognizes that, behind everything else, is the economic problem.

Aside from the personal and business interest which he has in the growth and progress of Mound Bayou, Mr. Banks sees in it a means of teaching better methods of farming, of improving the home life, of getting into the masses of the people greater sense of the value of law and order.

I have learned much from studying the success of Charles Banks. Before all else he has taught me the value of common sense in dealing with conditions as they exist in the south. I have learned from him that, in spite of what the Southern white man may say about the Negro in moments of excitement, the sober sentiment of the South is in sympathy with every effort that promises solid and substantial progress to the Negro.

Maj. R. R. Moton, of Hampton Institute, is one of the few black men I know who can trace his ancestry in an unbroken line on both sides back to Africa. I have often heard him tell the story, as he had it from his grandmother, of the way in which his great-grandfather, who was a young African chief, had come down to the coast to sell some captives taken in war and how, after the bargain was completed, he was enticed on board the white man's ship and himself carried away and sold, along with these unfortunate captives, into slavery in America. Major Moton is, like Charles Banks, not only a full-blooded black man, with a big body and broad negro features, but he is, in his own way, a remarkably handsome man. I do not think anyone could look in Major Moton's face without liking him. In the first place, he looks straight at you, out of big friendly eyes, and as he speaks to you an expression of alert and intelligent sympathy constantly flashes and plays across his kindly features.

It has been my privilege to come into contact with many different types of people, but I know few men who are so lovable and, at the same time, so sensible in their nature as Major Moton. He is chock-full of common sense. Further than that, he is a man who, without obtruding himself and without your understanding how he does it, makes you believe in him from the very first time you see him and from your first contact with him, and, at the same time, makes you love him. He is the kind of man in whose company I always feel like being, never tire of, always want to be around him, or always want to be near him.

One of the continual sources of surprise to people who come for the first time into the Southern States is to hear of the affection with which white men and women speak of the older generation of coloured people with whom they grew up, particularly the old coloured nurses. The lifelong friendships that exist between these old "aunties" and "uncles" and the white children with whom they were raised is something that is hard for strangers to understand.

It is just these qualities of human sympathy and affection that endeared so many of the older generation of Negroes to their masters and mistresses and which seems to have found expression, in a higher form, in Major Moton. Although he has little schooling outside of what he was able to get at Hampton Institute, Major Moton is one of the best-read men and one of the most interesting men to talk with I have ever met. Education has not "spoiled" him, as it seems to have done in the case of some other educated Negroes. It has not embittered or narrowed him in his affections. He has not learned to hate or distrust any class of people, and he is just as ready to assist and show a kindness to a white man as to a black man, to a Southerner as to a Northerner.

My acquaintance with Major Moton began, as I remember, after he had graduated at Hampton Institute and while he was employed there as a teacher. He had at that time the position that I once occupied in charge of the Indian students. Later he was given the very responsible position he now occupies, at the head of the institute battalion, as commandant of cadets, in which he has charge of the discipline of all the students. In this position he has an opportunity to exert a very direct and personal influence upon the members of the student body and, what is especially important, to prepare them to meet the peculiar difficulties that await them when they go out in the world to begin life for themselves.

It has always seemed to me very fortunate that Hampton Institute should have had in the position which Major Moton occupies a man of such kindly good humour, thorough self-control, and sympathetic disposition.

Major Moton knows by intuition Northern white people and Southern white people. I have often heard the remark made that the Southern white man knows more about the Negro in the South than anybody else. I will not stop here to debate that question, but I will add that coloured men like Major Moton know more about the Southern white man than anybody else on earth.

At the Hampton Institute, for example, they have white teachers and coloured teachers; they have Southern white people and Northern white people; besides, they have coloured students and Indian students. Major Moton knows how to keep his hands on all of these different elements, to see to it that friction is kept down and that each works in harmony with the other. It is a difficult job, but Major Moton knows how to negotiate it.

This thorough understanding of both races which Major Moton possesses has enabled him to give his students just the sort of practical and helpful advice and counsel that no white man who has not himself faced the peculiar conditions of the Negro could be able to give.

THE NEED FOR HEROES

I think it would do any one good to attend one of Major Moton's Sunday-school classes when he is explaining to his students, in the very practical way which he knows how to use, the mistake of students allowing themselves to be embittered by injustice or degraded by calumny and abuse with which every coloured man must expect to meet at one time or another. Very likely he will follow up what he has to say on this subject by some very apt illustration from his own experience or from that of some of his acquaintances which will show how much easier and simpler it is to meet prejudice with sympathy and understanding than with hatred; to remember that the man who abuses you because of your race probably hasn't the slightest knowledge of you personally, and, nine times out of ten, if you simply refuse to feel injured by what he says, will feel ashamed of himself later.

I think one of the greatest difficulties which a Negro has to meet is in travelling about the country on the railway trains. For example, it is frequently difficult for a coloured man to get anything to eat while he is travelling in the South, because, on the train and at the lunch counters along the route, there is often no provision for coloured people. If a coloured man goes to the lunch counter where the white people are served he is very likely, no matter who he may be, to find himself roughly ordered to go around to the kitchen, and even there no provision has been made for him.

Time and again I have seen Major Moton meet this situation, and others like it, by going up directly to the man in charge and telling him what he wanted. More than likely the first thing he received was a volley of abuse. That never discouraged Major Moton. He would not allow himself to be disturbed nor dismissed, but simply insisted, politely and good-naturedly, that he knew the custom, but that he was hungry and wanted something to eat. Somehow, without any loss of dignity, he not only invariably got what he wanted, but after making the man he was dealing with ashamed of himself, he usually made him his friend and left him with a higher opinion of the Negro race as a whole.

I have seen Major Moton in a good many trying situations in which an ordinary man would have lost his head, but I have never seen

59

him when he seemed to feel the least degraded or humiliated. I have learned from Major Moton that one need not belong to a superior race to be a gentleman.

It has been through contact with men like Major Moton—clean, wholesome, high-souled gentlemen under black skins—that I have received a kind of education no books could impart. Whatever disadvantages one may suffer from being a part of what is called an "inferior race," a member of such a race has the advantage of not feeling compelled to go through the world, as some members of other races do, proclaiming their superiority from the house tops. There are some people in this world who would feel lonesome, and they are not all of them white people either, if they did not have someone to whom they could claim superiority.

One of the most distinguished black men of my race is **George W. Clinton,** of Charlotte, N. C., bishop of the A. M. E. Zion Church. Bishop Clinton was born a slave fifty years ago in South Carolina. He was one of the few young coloured men who, during the Reconstruction days, had an opportunity to attend the University of South Carolina. He prides himself on the fact that he was a member of that famous class of 1874 which furnished one Negro congressman, two United States ministers to Liberia—the most recent of whom is Dr. W. D. Crum—five doctors, seven preachers, and several business men who have made good in after life. Among others was W. McKinlay, the present collector of customs for the port of Georgetown, D. C.

RUFUS HERRON
OF CAMP HILL, ALA.

"If there is a white man, North or South, that has more love for his community or his country than Rufus Herron, it has not been my good fortune to meet him"

MAJOR ROBERT RUSSA MOTON

"It has been through contact with men like Major Moton that I have received a kind of education no books could impart"

PROFESSOR GEORGE WASHINGTON CARVER

"One of the most thoroughly scientific men of the Negro race"

BISHOP GEORGE W. CLINTON

"He is the kind of man who wins everywhere confidence and respect"

Bishop Clinton has done a great service to the denomination to which he belongs and his years of service have brought him many honours and distinctions. He founded the *African Methodist Episcopal Zion Quarterly Review* and edited, for a time, another publication of the African Methodist Episcopal Zion denomination. He has represented his church in ecumenical conferences at home and abroad, is a trustee of Livingstone College, chairman of the publishing board, has served as a member of the international convention of arbitration and is vice-president of the international Sunday-school union.

Bishop Clinton is a man of a very different type from the other men of pure African blood I have mentioned. Although he says he is fifty years of age, he is in appearance and manner the youngest man in the group. An erect, commanding figure, with a high, broad forehead, rather refined features and fresh, frank, almost boyish manner, he is the kind of man who everywhere wins confidence and respect.

Although Bishop Clinton is by profession a minister, and has been all his life in the service of the Church, he is of all the men I have named the most aggressive in his manner and the most soldierly in his bearing.

Knowing that his profession compelled him to travel about a great deal in all parts of the country, I asked him how a man of his temperament managed to get about without getting into trouble.

"I have had some trouble but not much," he said, "and I have learned that the easiest way to get along everywhere is to be a gentleman. It is simple, convenient, and practicable.

"The only time I ever came near having any serious trouble," continued Bishop Clinton, "was years ago when I was in politics." And then he went on to relate the following incident: It seems that at this time the Negroes at the bishop's home in Lancaster, S. C., were still active in politics. There was an attempt at one time to get some of the better class of Negroes to unite with some of the Democrats in order to elect a prohibition ticket. The fusion ticket, with two Negroes and four white men as candidates, was put in the field and elected. It turned out, however, that a good many white people cut the Negroes on the ticket and, at the same time, a good many Negroes cut the whites, so that there was some bad blood on both sides. A man who was the editor of the local paper at that time had accused young Clinton of having advised the Negroes to cut the fusion ticket.

"As I knew him well," said the bishop, "I went up to his office to explain. Some rather foolish remark I made irritated the editor and he jumped up and came toward me with a knife in his hands."

The bishop added that he didn't think the man really meant anything "because my mother used to cook in his family" and they had known each other since they were boys, so he simply took hold of his wrists and held them. The bishop is a big, stalwart, athletic man with hands that grip like a vice. He talked very quietly and they settled the matter between them.

Bishop Clinton has told me that he has made many lifelong friends among the white people of South Carolina, but this was the only time that he ever had anything like serious trouble with a white man.

I first made the acquaintance of Bishop Clinton when he came to Tuskegee in 1893 as representative of the African Methodist Episcopal Zion Church, at the dedication of the Phelps Hall Bible training school. The next year he came to Tuskegee as one of the lecturers in that school and he has spent some time at Tuskegee every year since then, assisting in the work of that institution.

Bishop Clinton has been of great assistance to us, not only in our work at Tuskegee, but in the larger work we have been trying to do in arousing interest throughout the country in Negro public schools. He organized and conducted through North Carolina in 1910 what I think was the most successful educational campaign I have yet been able to make in any of the Southern States.

Although he is an aggressive churchman, Bishop Clinton has found time to interest himself in everything that concerns the welfare of the Negro race. He is as interested in the business and economic as he is in the intellectual advancement of the race.

One of the most gifted men of the Negro race whom I ever happened to meet is **George W. Carver,** Professor Carver, as he is called at Tuskegee, where he has for many years been connected with the scientific and experimental work in agriculture carried on in connection with the Tuskegee Institute. I first met Mr. Carver about 1895 or 1896 when he was a student at the State Agricultural College at Ames, Iowa. I had heard of him before that time through Hon. James Wilson, now secretary of agriculture, who was for some time one of Mr. Carver's teachers. It was about this time that an attempt was made to put our work in agriculture on a scientific basis, and Mr. Carver was induced to come to Tuskegee to take charge of that work and of the state experiment station that had been established in connection with it. He has been doing valuable work in that department ever since and, as a result of his work in breeding cotton and of the bulletins he has prepared on experiments in building up worn-out soils, he has become widely known to both coloured and white farmers throughout the South.

When some years ago the state secretary of agriculture called a meeting at Montgomery of the leading teachers of the state, Professor Carver was the only coloured man invited to that meeting. He was at that time invited to deliver an address to the convention and for an hour was questioned on the interesting work he was doing at the experiment station.

Professor Carver, like the other men I have mentioned, is of unmixed African blood, and is one of the most thoroughly scientific men of the Negro race with whom I am acquainted. Whenever anyone who takes a scientific interest in cotton growing, or in the natural history of this part of the world, comes to visit Tuskegee, he invariably seeks out and consults Professor Carver. A few years ago the colonial secretary of the German empire, accompanied by one of the cotton experts of his department, travelling through the South in a private car, paid a visit of several days to Tuskegee largely to study, in connection with the other work of the school, the cotton-growing experiments that Professor Carver has been carrying on for some years.

In his book, "The Negro in the New World," Sir Harry Johnston, who has himself been much interested in the study of plant life in different parts of the world, says: "Professor Carver, who teaches scientific agriculture, botany, agricultural chemistry, etc., at Tuskegee, is, as regards complexion and features, an absolute Negro; but in the cut of his clothes, the accent of his speech, the soundness of his science, he might be professor of botany, not at Tuskegee, but at Oxford or Cambridge. Any European botanist of distinction, after ten minutes' conversation with this man, instinctively would treat him as a man on a level with himself."

What makes all that Professor Carver has accomplished the more remarkable is the fact that he was born in slavery and has had relatively few opportunities for study, compared with those which a white man who makes himself a scholar in any particular branch of science invariably has.

Professor Carver knows but little of his parentage. He was born on the plantation of a Mr. Carver in Missouri sometime during the war.

It was a time when it was becoming very uncomfortable to hold slaves in Missouri and so he and his mother were sent south into Arkansas. After the war Mr. Carver, the master, sent south to inquire what had become of his former slaves. He learned that they had all disappeared with the exception of a child, two or three years old, by the name of George, who was near dead with the whooping-cough and of so little value that the people in Arkansas said they would be very glad to get rid of him.

George was brought home, but he proved to be such a weak and sickly little creature that no attempt was made to put him to work and he was allowed to grow up among chickens and other animals around the servants' quarters, getting his living as best he could.

The little black boy lived, however, and he used his freedom to wander about in the woods, where he soon got on very good terms with all the insects and animals in the forest and gained an intimate and, I might almost say personal, acquaintance with all the plants and the flowers.

As he grew older he began to show unusual aptitude in two directions: He attracted attention, in the first place, by his peculiar knack and skill in all sorts of household work. He learned to cook, to knit and crochet, and he had a peculiar and delicate sense for colour. He learned to draw and, at the present time, he devotes a large part of his leisure to making the most beautiful and accurate drawings of different flowers and forms of plant life in which he is interested.

In the second place, he showed a remarkable natural aptitude and intelligence in dealing with plants. He would spend hours, for example, gathering all the most rare and curious flowers that were to be found in the woods and fields. One day someone discovered that he had established out in the brush a little botanical garden, where he had gathered all sorts of curious plants and where he soon became so expert in making all sorts of things grow, and showed such skill in caring for and protecting plants from all sorts of insects and diseases that he got the name of "the plant doctor."

Another direction in which he showed unusual natural talent was in music. While he was still a child he became famous among the coloured people as a singer. After he was old enough to take care of himself he spent some years wandering about. When he got the opportunity he worked in greenhouses. At one time he ran a laundry; at another time he worked as a cook in a hotel. His natural taste and talent for music and painting, and, in fact, almost every form of art, finally attracted the attention of friends, through whom he secured a position as church organist.

During all this time young Carver was learning wherever he was able. He learned from books when he could get them; learned from experience always; and made friends wherever he went. At last he found an opportunity to take charge of the greenhouses of the horticultural department of the Iowa Agricultural College at Ames. He remained there until he was graduated, when he was made assistant botanist. He took advantage of his opportunities there to continue his studies and finally took a diploma as a post-graduate student, the first diploma of that sort that had been given at Ames.

While he was at the agricultural college in Iowa he took part with the rest of the students in all the activities of college life. He was lieutenant, for example, in the college battalion which escorted

Governor Boies to the World's Fair at Chicago. He began to read papers and deliver lectures at the horticultural conventions in all parts of the state. But, in spite of his success in the North, among the people of another race, Mr. Carver was anxious to come South and do something for his own race. So it was that he gladly accepted an invitation to come to Tuskegee and take charge of the scientific and experimental work connected with our department of agriculture.

Although Professor Carver impresses everyone who meets him with the extent of his knowledge in the matter of plant life, he is quite the most modest man I have ever met. In fact, he is almost timid. He dresses in the plainest and simplest manner possible; the only thing that he allows in the way of decoration is a flower in his button-hole. It is a rare thing to see Professor Carver any time during the year without some sort of flower on the lapel of his coat, and he is particularly proud when he has found somewhere in the woods some especially rare specimen of a flower to show to his friends.

I asked Professor Carver at one time how it was, since he was so timid, that he managed to have made the acquaintance of so many of the best white as well as coloured people in our part of the country. He said that as soon as people found out that he knew something about plants that was valuable he discovered they were very willing and eager to talk with him.

"But you must have some way of advertising," I said jestingly; "how do all these people find out that you know about plants?"

"Well, it is this way," he said. "Shortly after I came here I was going along the woods one day with my botany can under my arm. I was looking for plant diseases and for insect enemies. A lady saw what she probably thought was a harmless old coloured man, with a strange looking box under his arm, and she stopped me and asked if I was a peddler. I told her what I was doing. She seemed delighted and asked me to come and see her roses, which were badly diseased. I showed her just what to do for them—in fact, sat down and wrote it out for her.

"In this," he continued, "and several other ways it became noised abroad that there was a man at the school who knew about plants. People began calling upon me for information and advice."

I myself recall that several years ago a dispute arose down town about the name of a plant. No one knew what it was. Finally one gentleman spoke up and said that they had a man out at the normal school by the name of Carver who could name any plant, tree, bird, stone, etc., in the world, and if he did not know there was no use to look farther. A man was put on a horse and the plant brought to Professor Carver at the Institute. He named it and sent him back. Since then Professor Carver's laboratory has never been free from specimens of some kind.

I have always said that the best means which the Negro has for destroying race prejudice is to make himself a useful and, if possible, an indispensable member of the community in which he lives. Every man and every community is bound to respect the man or woman who has some form of superior knowledge or ability, no matter in what direction it is. I do not know of a better illustration of this than may be found in the case of Professor Carver. Without any disposition to push himself forward into any position in which he is not wanted, he has been able, because of his special knowledge and ability, to make friends with all classes of people, white as well as black, throughout the South. He is constantly receiving inquiries in regard to his work from all parts of the world, and his experiments in breeding new varieties of cotton have aroused the greatest interest among those cotton planters who are interested in the scientific investigation of cotton growing.

There are few coloured men in the South to-day who are better or more widely known than **Dr. Charles T. Walker,** pastor of the Tabernacle Baptist Church of Augusta, Georgia, President William H. Taft, referring to Doctor Walker, said that he was the most eloquent man he had ever listened to. For myself I do not know of any man, white or black, who is a more fascinating speaker either in private conversation or on the public platform.

Doctor Walker's speeches, like his conversation, have the charm of a natural-born talker, a man who loves men, and has the art of expressing himself simply, easily, and fluently, in a way to interest and touch them.

On the streets of Augusta, his home, it is no uncommon thing to see Doctor Walker—after the familiar and easy manner of Southern people—stand for hours on a street corner or in front of a grocery store, surrounded by a crowd who have gathered for no other purpose than to hear what he will say. It is said that he knows more than half of the fifteen thousand coloured people of Augusta by name, and when he meets any of them in the street he is disposed to stop, in his friendly and familiar way, in order to inquire about the other members of the family. He wants to know how each is getting on and what has happened to any one of them since he saw them last.

If one of these acquaintances succeeds in detaining him, he will, very likely, find himself surrounded by other friends and acquaintances and, when once he is fairly launched on one of the quaintly humorous accounts of his adventures in some of the various parts of the world he has visited, or is discussing, in his vivid and epigrammatic way, some public question, business in that part of the town stops for a time.

Doctor Walker is a great story teller. He has a great fund of anecdotes and a wonderful art in using them to emphasize a point in argument or to enforce a remark. I recall that the last time he was at Tuskegee, attending the Negro conference, he told us what he was trying to do at the school established by the Walker Baptist Association at Augusta for the farmers in his neighbourhood. From that he launched off into some remarks upon the coloured farmer, his opportunities, and his progress. He said Senator Tillman[3] had once complained that the coloured farmer wasn't as ignorant as he pretended to be, and then he told this story: He said that an old coloured farmer in his part of the

---

[3] A Democrat from South Carolina, Benjamin "Pitchfork Ben" Tillman was a White supremacist who advocating lynching Black people to make them "learn their place." –Ed.

country had rented some land of a white man on what is popularly known as "fourths." By the term of the contract the white man was to get one fourth of the crop for the use of the land.

When it came time to divide the crop, however, it turned out that there were just three wagon loads of cotton and this the old farmer hauled to his own barn.

Of course the landlord protested. He said: "Look here, Uncle Joe, didn't you promise me a fourth of that cotton for my share?"

"Yes, cap'n," was the reply, "Dat's so. I'se mighty sorry, but dere wasn't no fort'."

"How is that?" inquired the landlord.

"There wasn't no fort' 'cause dere was just three wagon loads, and dere wasn't no fort' dere."

Doctor Walker is not only a fascinating conversationalist, a warm-hearted friend, but he is, also, a wonderfully successful preacher. During the time when he was in New York, as pastor of the Mt. Olivet Baptist Church, his sermons and his wonderful success as an evangelist were frequently reported in the New York papers.

Doctor Walker is not only an extraordinary pulpit orator, but he is a man of remarkably good sense. I recall some instances in particular in which he showed this quality in a very conspicuous way. The first was at a meeting of the National Convention of Negro Baptists at St. Louis in 1886. At this meeting someone delivered an address on the subject, "Southern Ostracism," in which he abused the Southern white Baptists, referring to them as mere figureheads, who believe "there were separate heavens for white and coloured people."

Later in the session Doctor Walker found an opportunity to reply to these remarks, pointing out that a few months before the Southern Baptist Convention had passed a resolution to expend $10,000 in mission work among the coloured Baptists of the South. He formulated his protest against the remarks made by the speaker of the previous day in a resolution which was passed by the convention.

His speech and the resolution were published in many of the Southern newspapers and denominational organs and did much to change the currents of popular feeling at that time and bring about a better understanding between the races.

A MEETING OF THE NEGRO MINISTERS OF MACON COUNTY, ALABAMA

Dr. Charles T. Walker was born at the little town of Hepzibah, Richmond County, Ga., about sixteen miles south of his present home, Augusta. His father, who was his master's coachman, was also deacon in the little church organized by the slaves in 1848, of which his uncle was pastor. Doctor Walker comes of a race of preachers. The Walker Baptist Association is named after one of his uncles, Rev. Joseph T. Walker, whose freedom was purchased by the members of his congregation who were themselves slaves. In 1880, upon a resolution of Doctor Walker, this same Walker Association passed a resolution to establish a normal school for coloured children, known as the Walker Baptist Institute. This school has from the first been supported by the constant and unremitting efforts of Doctor Walker.

Meanwhile he has been interested in other good works. He assisted in establishing the Augusta *Sentinel*, and in 1891, while he was travelling in the Holy Land, his accounts of his travels did much to brighten its pages and increase its circulation.

In 1893 he was one of a number of other coloured people to establish a Negro state fair at Augusta, which has continued successfully ever since. Another of his enterprises started and carried on in connection with his church is the Tabernacle Old Folks' Home. He has taken a prominent part in all the religious and educational work of the state and has even dipped, to some extent, into politics, having been at one time a member of the Republican state executive committee.

Aside from these manifold activities, and beyond all he has done in other directions, Doctor Walker has been a man who has constantly sought to take life as he found it and make the most of the opportunities that he saw about him for himself and his people. He has not been an agitator and has done more than any other man I know to bring about peace and good-will between the two sections of the country and the races. It is largely due to his influence that in Augusta, Ga., the black man and the white man live more happily and comfortably than they do in almost any other city in the United States.

THE NEED FOR HEROES

The motto of Doctor Walker's life I can state in his own words. "I am determined," he has said, "never to be guilty of ingratitude; never to desert a friend; and never to strike back at an enemy."

It is because of such men as Doctor Walker and many others like him that I have learned not only to respect but to take pride in the race to which I belong.

In seeking to answer the question as to the relative value of the man of pure African extraction and the man of mixed blood I have referred to five men who have gained some distinction in very different walks of life. There are hundreds of others I could name, who, though not so conspicuous nor so well known, are performing in their humble way valuable service for their race and country. I might also mention here the fact that at Tuskegee, during an experience of thirty years, we have found that, although perhaps a majority of our students are not of pure black blood, still the highest honours in our graduating class, namely, that of valedictorian, which is given to students who have attained the highest scholarship during the whole course of their studies, has been about equally divided between students of mixed and pure blood.

For my own part, however, it seems to me a rather unprofitable discussion that seeks to determine in advance the possibilities of any individual or any race or class of individuals. In the first place, races, like individuals, have different qualities and different capacities for service and, that being the case, it is the part of wisdom to give every individual the opportunities for growth and development which will fit him for the greatest usefulness.

When any individual and any race is allowed to find that place, freely and without compulsion, they will not only be happy and contented in themselves, but will fall naturally into the happiest possible relations with all other members of the community.

In the second place, it should be remembered that human life and human society are so complicated that no one can determine what latent possibilities any individual or any race may possess. It is only through education, and through struggle and experiment in all the different activities and relations of life, that it is possible for a race or an individual to find the place in the common life in which they can be of the greatest value to themselves and the rest of the world.

To assume anything else is to deny the value of the free institutions under which we live and of all the centuries of struggle and effort it has cost to bring them into existence.

Fig. 3. Memorial to Robert Gould Shaw and the Massachusetts 54th Regiment, by Augustus Saint-Gaudens

ADDRESS FROM THE DEDICATION OF THE MEMORIAL TO ROBERT GOULD SHAW AND THE MASSACHUSETTS 54TH REGIMENT, MAY 30, 1897[4]

Mr. Chairman, and Fellow-Citizens: In this presence, and on this sacred and memorable day, in the deeds and death of our hero, we recall the old, old story, ever old, yet ever new, that when it was the will of the Father to lift humanity out of wretchedness and bondage, the precious task was delegated to him who among ten thousand was altogether lovely, and was willing to make himself of no reputation that he might save and lift up others.

If that heart could throb and if those lips could speak, what would be the sentiment and words that Robert Gould Shaw would have us feel and speak at this hour? He would not have us dwell long on the mistakes, the injustice, the criticisms of the days

"Of storm and cloud, of doubt and fears,
Across the eternal sky must lower;
Before the glorious noon appears."

He would have us bind up with his own undying fame and memory, and retain by the side of his monument, the name of John A. Andrew, who, with prophetic vision and strong arm helped make the existence of the 54th Regiment possible; and that of George L. Stearns, who, with hidden generosity and a great sweet heart, helped to turn the darkest hour into day, and in doing so freely gave service, fortune, and life itself to the cause which this day commemorates. Nor would he have

---

[4] In Rogers, *The Monument to Robert Gould Shaw*. This speech was reported in newspapers around the world. Famous for his oratory, Washington was said to have outshone all the other speakers, including William James —Ed.

us forget those brother officers, living and dead, who, by their baptism in blood and fire, in defence of union and freedom, gave us an example of the highest and purest patriotism.

To you who fought so valiantly in the ranks, the scarred and scattered remnant of the 54th Regiment, who with empty sleeve and wanting leg have honoured this occasion with your presence—to you, your commander is not dead. Though Boston erected no monument, and history recorded no story, in you and the loyal race which you represent, Robert Gould Shaw would have a monument which time could not wear away.

But an occasion like this is too great, too sacred, for mere individual eulogy. The individual is the instrument, national virtue the end. That which was three hundred years being woven into the warp and woof of our democratic institutions could not be effaced by a single battle, as magnificent as was that battle; that which for three centuries had bound master and slave, yea, North and South, to a body of death, could not be blotted out by four years of war, could not be atoned for by shot and sword, nor by blood and tears.

Not many days ago, in the heart of the South, in a large gathering of the people of my race, there were heard from many lips praises and thanksgiving to God for his goodness in setting them free from physical slavery. In the midst of that assembly a Southern white man arose, with gray hair and trembling hands, the former owner of many slaves, and from his quivering lips there came the words: "My friends, you forget in your rejoicing that in setting you free God was also good to me and my race in setting us free." But there is a higher and deeper sense in which both races must be free than that represented by the bill of sale. The black man who cannot let love and sympathy go out to the white man is but half free. The white man who would close the shop or factory against a black man seeking an opportunity to earn an honest living is but half free. The white man who retards his own development by opposing a black man is but half free. The full measure of the fruit of Fort Wagner and all that this monument stands for will not be realized until every man covered by a black skin shall, by patience and natural effort, grow to that height in industry, property, intelligence, and moral responsibility, where no man in all our land will be tempted to degrade himself by withholding from his black brother any opportunity which he himself would possess.

Until that time comes, this monument will stand for effort, not victory complete. What these heroic souls of the 54th Regiment began, we must complete. It must be completed not in malice, nor narrowness, nor artificial progress, nor in efforts at mere temporary political gain, nor in abuse of another section or race. Standing as I do to-day in the home of Garrison and Phillips and Sumner, my heart goes out to those who wore the gray as well as to those clothed in blue, to those who returned defeated to destitute homes, to face blasted hopes and a shattered political and industrial system. To them there can be no prouder reward for defeat than by a supreme effort to place the Negro on that footing where he will add material, intellectual, and civil strength to every department of state.

This work must be completed in public school, industrial school, and college. The most of it must be completed in the effort of the Negro himself; in his effort to withstand temptation, to economize, to exercise thrift, to disregard the superficial for the real, the shadow for the substance, to be great and yet small; in his effort to be patient in the laying of a firm foundation, to so grow in skill and knowledge that he shall place his services in demand by reason of his intrinsic and superior worth. This, this is the key that unlocks every door of opportunity, and all others fail. In this battle of peace, the rich and poor, the black and white may have a part.

What lesson has this occasion for the future? What of hope, what of encouragement, what of caution? "Watchman, tell us of the night, what the signs of promise are." If through me, an humble representative, nearly ten millions of my people might be permitted to send a message to Massachusetts, to the survivors of the 54th Regiment, to the committee whose untiring energy has made this memorial possible, to the family who gave their only boy that we might have life more abundantly, that message would be: Tell them that the sacrifice was not in vain, that up from the depths of ignorance and poverty we are coming, and if we come through oppression, out of the struggle we are gaining strength; by way of the school, the well-cultivated field, the skilled hand, the Christian home, we are coming up; that we propose to invite all who will to step up and occupy this position with us. Tell them that we are learning that standing ground for a race, as for an individual, must be laid in intelligence, industry, thrift, and property, not as an end, but as a means to the highest privileges; that we are learning that neither the conqueror's bullet, nor fiat of law, could make an ignorant voter an intelligent voter, could make a dependent man an independent man, could give one citizen respect for another, a bank account, a foot of land, or an enlightened fireside. Tell them that, as grateful as we are to artist and patriotism for placing the figures of Shaw and his comrades in physical form of beauty and magnificence, that after all the real monument, the greater monument, is being slowly but safely builded among the lowly in the South, in the address by struggles and sacrifices of a race to justify all that has been done and suffered for it.

One of the wishes that lay nearest to Colonel Shaw's heart was, that his black troops might be permitted to fight by the side of white soldiers. Have we not lived to see that wish realized, and will it not be more so in the future? Not at Wagner, not with rifle and bayonet, but on the field of peace, in the battle of industry, in the struggle for good government, in the lifting up of the lowest to the fullest opportunities. In this we shall fight by the side of white men North and South. And if this be true, as under God's guidance it will, that old flag, that emblem of progress and security which brave Sergeant Carney never permitted to fall upon the ground, will still be borne aloft by Southern soldier and Northern soldier, and in a more potent and higher sense we shall all realize that

> "The slave's chain and the master's alike are broken;
> The one curse of the race held both in tether;
> They are rising,—all are rising,
> The black and white together!"

78

5. Carter G. Woodson

ARMING BLACK SOLDIERS
DURING THE
U.S. CIVIL WAR[1]

Northern men like General DePeyster, General Thomas W. Sherman, general Hunter, Governor Yates of Illinois, Henry Wilson, and Charles Sumner, had been emphatic in urging the United States government to arm the Negroes to weaken the South. And well might the United States Army take this action, for the seceders had

---

[1] Extract from *The Negro in Our History*, pp 231-238.

not only made use of the Negroes as labourers, but in Tennessee and Louisiana had actually organized free Negroes for military service in the Confederate Army. Yet, although the confiscation acts and other legislation justified the employment of Negroes, Lincoln hesitated to carry out these provisions. In 1862, however, General David Hunter, commanding in South Carolina, issued an order for recruiting a Negro regiment, which in a few months was in the field. This caused much dissatisfaction among the Unionists, who did not feel that Negroes should be called on to fight the battles of a free republic. An effort was made to embarrass General Hunter, but he emerged from the investigation without being reversed, although he did not have the support of Lincoln. General J. W. Phelps, under General B. F. Butler in Louisiana, undertook to carry out Hunter's policy, but his superior was then willing to use the Negroes as labourers only.

Certain leaders in the North, however, were becoming a little more aggressive in their demand for the employment of Negroes as soldiers. On August 4, 1862, Governor Sprague of Rhode Island urged Negro citizens to enlist, and that same month Butler himself appealed to the free people of colour of Louisiana to come to the defence of the Union. The next month a regiment of Negroes marched forth to war as the "First Regiment of Louisiana Native Guards," soon changed to the "First Regiment Infantry Corps d'Afrique." There was later organized the "First Regiment Louisiana Heavy Artillery." Other Negro regiments soon followed, and before the end of 1862 four Negro regiments had been brought into the military service of the United States. Then came the "Kansas Coloured Volunteers" early in 1863, and when the Emancipation Proclamation had been signed Lincoln officially authorized the raising of Negro troops. Then followed the famous Fifty-fourth Massachusetts and so many other troops that there was established in Washington a special bureau for handling affairs respecting these units, aggregating before the end of the war 178,975.

In keeping with the custom which was all but followed during the World War, the Negro troops were commanded most altogether by white officers. There was some doubt that the Negro would make a good soldier and, of course, the Negro officer was then almost impossible. Massachusetts, however, commissioned ten Negro officers, Kansas three, and the military authorities a considerable number in Louisiana. Negroes held altogether about seventy-five commissions in the army during the Civil War. Among these officers were Lieutenant Colonel William N. Reed of the First North Carolina, a man well educated in Germany. He made a gallant charge with his regiment at the battle of Olustee, Florida, where he was mortally wounded. In the Kansas corps, there were Captain H. Ford Douglass, First Lieutenant W. D. Matthews and Second Lieutenant Patrick A. Minor. In the USCT 104th regiment there were Major Martin R. Delaney and Captain O. S. B. Wall of Company K. Doctor Alexander T. Augusta, who was surgeon of the USCT 7th regiment, was finally breveted with Lieutenant-Colonel . Doctor John V. DeGrasse was assistant surgeon of the USCT 35th regiment. Charles B. Purvis, Alpheus Tucker, John Rapier, William Ellis, Anderson R. Abbott and William Powell were hospital surgeons at Washington, DC.

One might inquire, too, as to exactly what was the status of the Negro troops. In the first place, they were not treated as the equals of white men. There was objection to giving them the same compensation offered the whites. In the matter of bounties there was a discrimination against Negro soldiers who were slaves on April 19, 1861. This caused dissatisfaction among the Negro troops, whose families thereby seriously suffered. Sergeant William Walker was shot by order of court martial because he had his company stack arms before the captain's tent for the reason that the Government had failed to comply with its contract. The 54th of Massachusetts nobly refused to receive its pay until it had been made equal to that of the whites. Negro troops, moreover, were often used by white troops for fatigue duty. Because of this notorious discrimination many of these soldiers became restive, sullen and even insubordinate.

Yet these Negroes distinguished themselves as soldiers. Men under whom these troops fought in battle were loud and praise of their gallantry and martyrdom. Negroes served in almost all parts of the South.

They engaged in the perilous South Edisto expedition to burn a bridge above Walton Bluff to aid General Sherman, and participated in the action at Honey Hill. Speaking of their behaviour in the expedition to Derby River in Georgia, General Rufus Saxon said that they fought with most determined bravery. Surgeon Seth Rogers, operating in South Carolina, said that braver men never lived. Colonel T. W. Higginson himself believed that "It would have been madness to attempt with the bravest white troops what he successfully accomplished with the black." Even in the failure to carry Fort Wagner, a point necessary to the capture of Charleston, the Negro troops bore the severest test of valour, following the gallant leader, Colonel Robert Gould Shaw, who in this charge fell mortally wounded.

In the Mississippi Valley they fought still more bravely. Negro troops made six such desperate charges on a fort at Port Hudson that a reporter said that the deeds of heroism performed by these black men were such as the proudest white men might emulate. General banks said in referring to their behaviour: "It gives me great pleasure to report that they answered every expectation. Their conduct was heroic; no troops could be more determined or more daring." Other troops from Louisiana showed themselves equally brave at Milliken's Bend. Reporting this battle, Captain Matthew M. Miller said: "So they fought and died, defending the cause that we revere. They met death coolly, bravely; nor rashly did they expose themselves, but always steady and obedient to orders." And so went others to death in the massacre at Fort Pillow in Tennessee, where the Confederates, in keeping with their bold declaration not to give quarter to the slaves striking for their own freedom, slaughtered them as men kill beasts.

In the Department of the Potomac the Negro maintained there his reputation as a soldier. Under General Wild, at Fort Powhattan in 1864, the Negro soldiers bravely held their ground against the heavy onslaught of Fitzhugh Lee's brilliant soldiers, who were badly worsted in the conflict. When General Grant was endeavouring to reduce Petersburg, a brigade of Hinck's Negro division brilliantly dashed forward and cleared a line of rifle-pits and carried a redoubt ahead. They did valiant work of the same order at South Mountain and died bravely in carrying the fortified positions of the Confederates at New Market Heights and nearer to Petersburg. In the dash along the James and in the pursuit of Lee's weakened forces, the Negroes under arms maintained their bearing as brave men and came out of the Civil War as heroes.

Fig. 4. Memorial to Robert Gould Shaw and the Massachusetts 54th Regiment, by Augustus Saint-Gaudens (detail)

5. CARTER G. WOODSON

PALMARES[2]

…This better situation of a few Negroes was due also to the fact that a large number of slaves in remote parts of the West Indies and Latin America asserted themselves and **The Maroons** escaped to uninhabited districts to declare and maintain their independence rather than bear the yoke of bondage. In parts where the Negroes were as numerous as the whites, these fugitives often jeopardized the very life of the colony. As such, they were known as maroons. They had few arms that the primitive man did not possess, but because of their resourcefulness and power in military organization they became a source of much terror throughout Latin America. In the small colony of Guatemala in the seventeenth century there were as many as three hundred such Negroes who had resorted to the woods and could not be subdued by the forces sent against them.

The greatest enterprise of the maroons, however, was exhibited not by any particular individual but rather by that of the little Negro Republic in Brazil, called Palmares, styled by Professor Charles E. Chapman as the Negro Numantia,[3] because its career resembles so much that of Numantia against which the Romans fought for a number of years before they could invade the beleaguered city. Because of the bad treatment of the Portuguese slaves, many of those imported from Guinea escaped to the forests, where they established villages called *quilombos,* the type to which Palmares, in the Province of Pernambuco, belonged. It was not long, however, before this town extended its sway over a number of other settled by persons of the same antecedents. At one time it was reported to have a population of twenty thousand, with ten thousand fighting men. Palmares, the name also of the capital of the republic, was surrounded by wooden walls made of the trunks of trees

---

[2] Extract from *The Negro in Our History*, pp. 30-33.
[3] Chapman, "Palmares: The Negro Numantia."

and entered by huge gates provided with facilities for wide surveillance and sentry service.

In the course of time the population of this village gradually increased because of the eagerness of slaves and freemen to try their fortunes in the forests. In the beginning they maintained themselves by a sort of banditry, taking food, slaves and women, whether mulatto, black, or white. They later settled down to agriculture, and established seemingly peaceful trade relations with the Portuguese settlements in the less hostile parts of Brazil. Palmares then developed into a sort of nation, uniting the desirable features of the republican and monarchical form of government, presided over by a chief executive called the *Zombe,* who ruled with absolute authority during life. "The right to candidacy," says Professor Chapman, "was restricted to a group recognized as composing the bravest men of the community. Any man in the state might aspire to this dignity providing he had Negro blood in his veins. There were other officers, both of a military and a civil character. In the interest of good order the *Zombes* made laws imposing the death penalty for murder, adultery and robbery. Influenced by their antecedents, slavery was not discontinued, but a premium was place on freedom in that every Negro who won his freedom by a successful flight to Palmares remained free, whereas those who were captured as slaves continued as such in Palmares."

This Negro Republic, however, was in the eyes of the Portuguese an unnatural growth. It was considered a resort for undesirable aliens who constituted an ever-increasing danger to the prosperity of Brazil. In 1698, therefore, Governor Caetano de Mello of Pernambuco ordered an expedition to proceed against the city. These brave blacks met the invading forces and indisputably defeated them. Returning later, however, with a formidable army of seven thousand men under the command of a more competent soldier and provided, too, with adequate artillery, the Portuguese reached the city after some difficulty and placed it in a state of siege. The defence of this city was heroic. "After the Portuguese had breached the walls in three places," says the annalist, "their infantry attacked in force. They entered the city, but had to take it foot by foot. At last the defenders came to the centre of Palmares where a high cliff impeded further retreat. Death or surrender were the only alternatives. Seeing that his cause was lost beyond repair, the *Zombe* hurled himself over the cliff, and his action was followed by the most distinguished of his fighting men. Some persons were indeed taken, but it is perhaps a tribute to Palmares, though a gruesome one, that they were all put to death; it was not safe to enslave these men, despite the value of their labour. Thus passed Palmares, the Negro Numantia, the most famous and greatest of the Brazilian quilombos."[4]

---

[4] *The Journal of Negro History,* vol. III, pp. 31-32. [Editor's note: More recent histories of Palmares, based on records left by the Portuguese victors, state that when "Zombe" or Zumbi was betrayed by one of his sons-in-law, the leader of Palmares died fighting on November 20, 1695, along with some twenty of his men. Zumbi's head was taken to the city of Recife, Pernambuco, and displayed on a wooden spike.]

6. J. A. Rogers

THE THRILLING STORY OF THE MAROONS[1]

Band of Heroic Negroes Defied the British Government for One Hundred and Fifty-one Years and Finally Forced It to Come to Terms; Maintained Their Independence with Arms and Ammunition Captured from the Oppressors.

The African, in spite of his great reputation for docility, did not everywhere submit calmly to slavery. In Cuba, Haiti, Porto Rico, Brazil, and even in the United States, where he was hopelessly

---

[1] Originally published in *Negro World* on March 18, 1922.

outnumbered, he would revolt from time to time. Then he would wreak terrible vengeance on his oppressors, slaying right and left like an enraged demon. In 1791 at Cape Francia, Haiti, the slaves revolted under Oge and wiped out the entire white colony, slaughtering men, women and children, and burning plantations with a ferocity paralleled only by the attacks of the Jews on the Canaanites[2] or of the mob on the nobility during the stirring time of the French Revolution. This phase of Haitian history has been graphically told by Victor Hugo in his powerful story, "Bug-Jargal."

The most refractory of all slaves, by far, were those on the Island of Jamaica. This, no doubt, was due to the fact that slaves always outnumbered the whites and near-whites by at least eight to one. The history of that island from its occupation by the British in 1655 to the Emancipation in 1838 is one long record of the attempts of those hot-headed blacks to gain their liberty. A large number of the Jamaican slaves were descendants of the Coromantin, [one of the] most warlike tribes of the West African coast.[3] The Coromantins refused to accept the religion of their masters, worshipping instead the terrible Obi [obeah]. Even after they were set free the Jamaican blacks revolted against unjust taxation. At Morant Bay in 1865 they attacked the officials in a court house, set fire to the building and gave the occupants the alternative of coming out to be shot or of being burned alive. Hundreds of blacks were wantonly killed in reprisal and their towns and villages destroyed wholesale, but the oppressors were taught a lesson. The almost total absence of racial friction on the island is due, perhaps, wholly to the determined stand the Jamaican black has always taken against unjust treatment.

Foremost of the insurrectionists were the Maroons, or hog-hunters. These blacks, whose name is still a by-word of dread, maintained an almost unbroken guerrilla warfare against the slaveholders for one hundred and forty-one years (1655-1796). When the African gets the recognition that is his in the history of the New World these

---

[2] Probably a reference to the Old Testament Book of Joshua –Ed.
[3] Now considered archaic, Coromantin or Coramantee was a British term for the Akan people of the Gold Coast, present-day Ghana –Ed.

primitive, untaught blacks in whose bosoms burned the inextinguishable fire of liberty, will be worshipped. They will be worshipped for their daring, their arduous feats, and the great privations they suffered in the cause of liberty. The Spartans, the Swiss mountaineers, the Scotch Highlanders, the American Colonists and the Belgians are today the leading idols of Western civilization. But these black men were the greater heroes, for while the American Colonists and all the others were on their own soil and free, these black men were not only escaped slaves, thousands of miles from their native land, but maintained their freedom solely by the arms and ammunition they took from their oppressors.

ORIGIN OF THE MAROONS

When the English captured Jamaica in 1655 from the Spaniards, the latter fled to Cuba, ninety miles away. In the flight they had to abandon the greater part of their slaves. Several hundreds of these took to the mountains, carrying with them food and clothing, arms and ammunition. Here they were joined from time to time by other runaways, where they became a perpetual thorn in the side of the English—the drop of gall in the enjoyment of this most beautiful and bountiful island. Jamaica is called "the black man's paradise." Its inhabitants are 85 per cent black. That this is so is due largely to the terror inspired in the hearts of perspective [sic] white settlers by the Maroons at the time when it was easiest for the white settlers to get on.

At first the Maroons roved in bands. Whenever they needed food, arms and clothing they would descend on the white settlers, and after plundering and killing in true Scotch Highlander fashion, would escape to their mountain fortresses. The island, though arable throughout, is very mountainous. Tradition says that Columbus, its discoverer, when asked by Ferdinand and Isabella for a description of it, took up a piece of paper, crumpled it in his hand and threw it on the table, saying "There it is."

Chief among the tormentors of the English at this period was a chief named St. Juan de Bolas. For eight years he ceaselessly harassed the whites, massacring settlement after settlement and preventing the advance of the planters. It must be remembered also that these blacks had been living on the island for more than a century and were fighting not only to prevent enslavement, but in defence of what they regarded [as] their native land. At last, worn out by age and fatigue, St. Juan de Bolas surrendered on a promise of freedom and land for himself and his followers.

The bands of the Maroons, however, refused to consider any terms. They continued their depredations being the terror of the slaveholders. It was almost impossible for the residents of the plantations to escape their attacks, as they would learn all their movements from the slaves, with whom they would mingle in the markets and other public places. Thus they knew the favourable moment to strike. Descending on a plantation they spared no white person or faithful slave. Toward the latter they were especially vindictive. After liberating the slaves, they took all the arms and the food, set fire to the plantation and retreated to the mountains.

After repeated attempts to defeat them had failed, the governor now resorted to conciliation. To each Maroon that would surrender he offered a sum of money and twenty acres of land. But the Maroons were already free and in possession of thousands of acres of the riches land and spurned his offers. At last, their old leader, St. Juan de Bolas, was persuaded to lead an expedition against them. He met with some success for a while, breaking up several bands, but at last he fell into a trap. His forces were cut to pieces and himself slain.

For the next ten years the Maroons continued their raids successfully preventing the spread of the white settlement in the interior of the island.

But soon a crisis came. The slaves in one of the parishes named Clavendon rebelled. Killing all their masters, they took arms and ammunition, including four field pieces, and joined the4 Maroons. At that time there were 8,000 whites, 80,000 slaves and a number of Indians on the island. The Maroons numbered about 900—men, women, and children.

Their numbers augmented, the Maroons became more daring and destructive than ever. The administration provoked beyond endurance decided to make war on them—resistance hitherto had been left to the planters themselves. A large expedition was assembled. Soldiers led by Indians and faithful slaves now succeeded in penetrating the retreats of many Maroon bands, killing and dispersing them.

The Maroons, up to this period, had been roving in bands. They now saw that safety lay in union, and concentrated their forces under one of the most daring and resourceful of their chiefs, a Coromantin named Cudjoe. Cudjoe appointed his two brothers, Johnny and Accompong, lieutenants, and made preparations for yet bolder attacks on the whites. In the words of [R. C.] Dallas, an Englishman, and a writer of those days, they began "a regular and connected system of warfare, and in their frequent skirmishes with the troops sent out against them, acquired an art of attack and defence, which, in the difficult and inaccessible fastnesses of the interior of the island, has since so often foiled the best exertions of disciplined bravery."[4] In nearly every encounter, Cudjoe was victorious and there is good reason to believe, that had he been better armed, he might, with the aid of the slaves, have eventually succeeded in driving out the English as a similar untaught Negro had forced the French from the neighbouring island of Haiti.

DESCRIPTION OF THE MAROONS

"In their person and carriage," says Dallas, in his *History of the Maroons*, "the Maroons were erect and lofty, indicating a consciousness of superiority; vigour, appeared upon their muscles, and their motions displayed agility. Their eyes were quick, wild and fiery, the white of them appearing a little red; owing, perhaps, to the greenness of the wood they burned in their houses…. They possessed most, if not all, of the senses in a superior degree. They were accustomed, from habit, to discover in the woods objects which white people of the best sight could not distinguish; and their hearing was so wonderfully quick that it enabled

---

[4] Dallas. *The History of the Maroons,* pp. 33-34.

them to elude their most active pursuers; they were seldom surprised. [In character, language and manners they nearly resembled those Negroes on the estates of the planters that were descended from the same race of Africans, but displayed a striking distinction in their personal appearance, being blacker, taller and in every respect handsomer.][5]

"They communicated with one another by means of horns, and when these could scarcely be heard by other people they distinguished the orders that the sounds conveyed. It is very remarkable that the Maroons had a particular call upon the horn for each individual by which he was summoned from a distance as easily as he would have been spoken to by name had he been near."[6]

---

[5] The sentence in brackets was inserted from pages 87-88 of Dallas, *The History of the Maroons* –Ed.
[6] Ibid., pp. 88-89.

7. W. E. B. Du Bois

From *THE GIFT OF BLACK FOLK*

CHAPTER III
Black Soldiers

How the Negro fought in every American war for a cause that was not his and to gain for others a freedom which was not his own.

1. COLONIAL WARS

The day is past when historians glory in war. Rather, with all thoughtful men, they deplore the barbarism of mankind which has made war so large a part of human history. As long, however, as there are powerful men who are determined to have their way by brute force, and as long as these men can compel or persuade enough of their group, nation or race to support them even to the limit of destruction, rape, theft and murder, just so long these men will and must be opposed by force—moral force if possible, physical force in the extreme. The world has undoubtedly come to the place where it defends reluctantly such defensive war, but has no words of excuse for offensive war, for the initiation of the program of physical force.

There is, however, one further consideration: the man in the ranks has usually little chance to decide whether the war is defensive or offensive, righteous or wrong. He is called upon to put life and limb in jeopardy. He responds, sometimes willingly with uplifted soul and high resolve, persuaded that he is under Divine command; sometimes by compulsion and by the iron of discipline. In all cases he has by every nation been given credit; and certainly the man who voluntarily lays down his life for a cause which he has been led to believe is righteous deserves public esteem, although the world may weep at his ignorance and blindness.

From the beginning America was involved in war because it was born in a day of war. First, there were wars, mostly of aggression but partly of self-defence, against the Indians. Then there was a series of wars which were but colonial echoes of European brawls. Next the United States fought to make itself independent of the economic suzerainty of England. After that came the conquest of Mexico and the war for the Union which resolved itself in a war against slavery, and finally the Spanish War and the great World War.

In all these wars the Negro has taken part. He cannot be blamed for them so far as they were unrighteous wars (and some of them were unrighteous), because he was not a leader: he was for the most part a common soldier in the ranks and did what he was told. Yet in the majority of cases he was not compelled to fight. He used his own judgment and he fought because he believed that by fighting for America he would gain the respect of the land and personal and spiritual freedom. His problem as a soldier was always peculiar: no matter for what America fought and no matter for what her enemies fought, the American Negro always fought for his own freedom and for the self-respect of his race. Whatever the cause of war, therefore, his cause was peculiarly just. He appears, therefore, in American wars always with double motive,—the desire to oppose the so-called enemy of his country along with his fellow white citizens, and before that, the motive of deserving well of those citizens and securing justice for his folk. In this way he appears in the earliest times fighting with the whites against the Indians as well as with the Indians against the whites, and throughout the history of the West Indies and Central America as well as the Southern United States we find here and there groups of Negroes fighting with the whites. For instance: in Louisiana early in the eighteenth century when Governor Perier took office, the colony was very much afraid of a combination between the Choctaw Indians and the fierce Banbara Negroes who had begun to make common cause with them. To offset this, Perier armed a band of slaves in 1729 and sent them against the Indians. He says: "The Negroes executed their mission with as much promptitude as secrecy." Later, in 1730, the Governor sent twenty white men and six Negroes to carry ammunition to the Illinois settlement up the Mississippi River. Perier says fifteen Negroes "in whose hands we had put weapons performed prodigies of valour. If the blacks did not cost so much and if their labour was not so necessary to the colony it would be better to turn them into soldiers and to dismiss those we have who are so bad and so cowardly that they seem to have been manufactured purposely for this colony." But this policy of using the Negroes against the Indians led the Indians to retaliate and seek alliance with the blacks and in August 1730, the Natchez Indians and the Chickshaws conspired with the Negroes to revolt. The head of the revolt, Samba, with eight of his confederates was executed before the conspiracy came to a head. In 1733, when Governor Bienville returned to power, he had an army consisting of 544 white men and 45 Negroes, the latter with free black officers.[1]

---

[1] Alice Dunbar Nelson, *Journal of Negro History,* vol. 1, pp 369, 370, 371.[Unless otherwise noted, all footnotes in this chapter are Du Bois's –Ed.]

7. W. E. B. Du Bois

In the colonial wars which distracted America during the seventeenth and early part of the eighteenth centuries the Negro took comparatively small part because the institution of slavery was becoming more settled and the masters were afraid to let their slaves fight. Notwithstanding this, there were black freedmen who voted and were enrolled in the militia and went to war, while some masters sent their slaves as labourers and servants. As early as 1652 a law of Massachusetts as to the militia required "Negro, Scotchmen and Indians" to enrol in the militia. Afterward the policy was changed and Negroes and Indians were excluded but Negroes often acted as sentinels at meeting-house doors. At other times slaves ran away and enlisted as soldiers or as sailors, thus often gaining their liberty. The New York *Gazette* in 1760 advertises for a slave who is suspected of having enlisted "in the provincial service." In 1763 the Boston *Evening Post* was looking for a Negro who "was a soldier last summer." One mulatto in 1746 is advertised for in the Pennsylvania *Gazette*. He had threatened to go to the French and Indians and fight for them. And in the Maryland *Gazette*, 1755, gentlemen are warned that their slaves may run away to the French and Indians.[2]

2. THE REVOLUTIONARY WAR

The estimates of the Negro soldiers who fought on the American side of the Revolutionary War vary from four to six thousand, or one out of every 50 or 60 of the colonial troops.

On August 24, 1778, the following report was made of Negroes in the Revolutionary Army:[3]

---

[2] Cf. Livermore, *Opinion of the Founders of the Republic,* etc., part 2; *Journal of Negro History,* vol. 1, p. 198 ff.
[3] G. H. Moore, *Historical Notes,* etc., N.Y., 1862.

Brigades	Present	Sick Absent	On Command	Total
North Carolina	42	10	6	58
Woodford	36	3	1	40
Muhlenburg	64	26	8	98
Smallwood	20	3	1	24
2nd Maryland	43	15	2	60
Wayne	2			2
2nd Pennsylvania	33	1	1	35
Clinton	33	2	4	62
Parsons	117	12	19	148
Huntington	56	2	4	62
Nixon	26		1	27
Paterson	64	13	12	89
Late Learned	34	4	8	46
Poor	16	7	4	27
Total	586	98	71	755

Alex. Scammell, Adj. Gen.

This report does not include Negro soldiers enlisted in Rhode Island, Connecticut, New York, New Hampshire and other States not mentioned nor does it include those who were in the army at both earlier and later dates. Other records prove that Negroes served in as many as eighteen brigades.

It was a Negro who in a sense began the actual fighting. In 1750 William Brown of Framingham, Mass., advertised three times for "A Molatto Fellow about 27 Years of Age, named *Crispas*, 6 Feet 2 Inches high, short Curl'd Hair." This runaway slave was the same Crispus Attucks who in 1779 led a mob on the 5th of March against the British soldiers in the celebrated "Boston Massacre."

Much has been said about the importance and lack of importance of this so-called "Boston Massacre." Whatever the verdict of history may be, there is no doubt that the incident loomed large in the eyes of the colonists. Distinguished men were orators on the 5th of March for years after, until that date was succeeded by the 4th of July.

Daniel Webster in his great Bunker Hill oration said: "From that moment we may date the severance of the British Empire."

Possibly these men exaggerated the actual importance of a street brawl between citizens and soldiers, led by a runaway slave; but there is no doubt that the colonists, who fought for independence from England, thought this occasion of tremendous importance and were nerved to great effort because of it.

Livermore says: "The presence of the British soldiers in King Street excited the patriotic indignation of the people. The whole community was stirred, and sage counsellors were deliberating and writing and talking about the public grievances. But it was not for the 'wise and prudent' to be first to act against the encroachments of arbitrary power. 'A motley rabble of saucy boys, Negroes and mulattoes, Irish Teagues and outlandish Jack tars,' (as John Adams described them in his plea in defence of the soldiers) could not restrain their emotion or stop to enquire if what they *must do* was according to the letter of the law. Led by Crispus Attucks, the mulatto slave, and shouting, 'The way to get rid of these soldiers is to attack the main guard; strike at the root; this is the nest'; with more valour than discretion they rushed to King Street and were fired upon by Captain Preston's company. Crispus Attucks was the first to fall; he and Samuel Gray and Jonas Caldwell were killed on the spot. Samuel Maverick and Patrick Carr were mortally wounded. The excitement which followed was intense. The bells of the town were rung. An impromptu town meeting was held and an immense assembly gathered. Three days after, on the 8th, a public funeral of the Martyrs took place. The shops in Boston were closed and all the bells of Boston and the neighbouring towns were rung. It is said that a greater number of persons assembled on this occasion than ever before gathered on this continent for a similar purpose. The body of Crispus Attucks, the mulatto, had been placed in Faneuil Hall with that of Caldwell, both being strangers in the city. Maverick was buried from his mother's house in Union Street, and Gray from his brother's in Royal Exchange Lane. The four hearses formed a junction in King Street and then the procession marched in columns six deep, with a long file of coaches belonging to the most distinguished citizens, to the Middle Burying Ground, where the four victims were deposited in one grave over which a stone was placed with the inscription:

'Long as in Freedom's cause the wise contend,
Dear to your country shall your fame extend;
While to the world the lettered stone shall tell
Where Caldwell, Attucks, Gray and Maverick fell.'

"The anniversary of this event was publicly commemorated in Boston by an oration and other exercises every year until our National Independence was achieved, when the Fourth of July was substituted for the Fifth of March as the more proper day for a general celebration. Not only was the event commemorated but the martyrs who then gave up their lives were remembered and honoured."[4]

The relation of the Negro to the Revolutionary War was peculiar. If his services were used by the Colonists this would be an excuse for the English to use the Indians and to emancipate the slaves. If he were not used not only was this source of strength to the small loyal armies neglected but there still remained the danger that the English would bid for the services of Negroes. At first then the free Negro went quite naturally into the army as he had for the most part been recognized as liable to military service. Then Congress hesitated and ordered that no Negroes be enlisted. Immediately there appeared the determination of the Negroes, whether deliberately arrived at or by the more or less unconscious development of thought under the circumstances, to give their services to the side which promised them freedom and decent treatment. When therefore Governor Dunmore of Virginia and English generals like Cornwallis and Clinton made a bid for the services of Negroes, coupled with promises of freedom, they got considerable numbers and in the case of Dunmore, one Negro unit fought a pitched battle against the Colonists.

---

[4] Livermore, pp. 115-16.

7. W. E. B. Du Bois

The Continental Congress took up the question of Negroes in the Army in September, 1775. A committee consisting of Lynch, Lee and Adams reported a letter which they had drafted to Washington. Rutledge of South Carolina moved that Washington be instructed to discharge all Negroes whether slave or free from the army, but this was defeated. October 8th Washington and other generals in council of war, agreed unanimously that slaves should be rejected and a large majority declared that they refuse free Negroes. October 18th, the question came up again before the committee consisting of Benjamin Franklin, General Washington, certain deputies, governors and others. This council agreed that Negroes should be rejected and Washington issued orders to this effect November 12th, 1775. Meantime, however, Dunmore's proclamation came and his later success in raising a black regiment which greatly disturbed Washington. In July, 1776, the British had 200 Negro soldiers on Long Island and later two regiments of Negroes were raised by the British in North Carolina. The South lost thousands of Negroes through the British. In Georgia a corps of fugitives calling themselves the "King of England Soldiers" kept attacking on both sides of the Savannah River even after the Revolution and many feared a general insurrection of slaves.[5]

The colonists soon began to change their attitude. Late in 1775, Washington reversed his decision and ordered his recruiting officers to accept free Negroes who had already served in the army and laid the matter before the Continental Congress. The Committee recommended that these Negroes be reenlisted but no others. Various leaders advised that it would be better to enlist the slaves, among them Samuel Hopkins, Alexander Hamilton, General Greene, James Madison. Even John Laurens of South Carolina tried to make the South accept the proposition.[6]

Thus Negroes again were received into the American army and from that time on they played important roles. They had already

---

[5] For more on this side of the story, see Simon Schama, *Rough Crossings* –Ed.
[6] Cf. Livermore and Moore, as above; also *Journal of Negro History,* Vol. 1, pp. 114-20.

distinguished themselves in individual cases at Bunker Hill. For instance, fourteen white officers sent the following statement to the Massachusetts Legislature on December 5, 1775: "The subscribers beg leave to report to your Honourable House (which we do in justice to the character of so brave a man) that under our own observation we declare that a Negro man named Salem Poor, of Colonel Frye's regiment, Captain Ames' company, in the late battle at Charlestown, behaved like an experienced officer as well as an excellent soldier. To set forth particulars of his conduct would be tedious. We only beg leave to say, in the person of this said Negro, centres a brave and gallant soldier. The reward due to so great and distinguished a character we submit to the Congress."[7]

They afterward fought desperately in Long Island and at the battle of Monmouth. Foreign travellers continually note the presence of Negroes in the American army.

Less known however is the help which the black republic of Haiti offered to the struggling Colonists. In December 1778 Savannah was captured by the British, and Americans were in despair until the French fleet appeared on the coast of Georgia in September 1779. The fleet offered to help recapture Savannah. It had on board 1900 French troops of whom 800 were black Haitian volunteers. Among these volunteers were Christophe, afterward king of Haiti, Rigaud, André, Lambert and others. They were a significant and faithful band which began by helping freedom in America, then turned and through the French revolution freed Haiti and finally helped in the emancipation of South America. The French troops landed below the city with the Americans at their right and together they made an attack. American and French flags were planted on the British outposts but their bearers were killed and a general retreat was finally ordered. Seven hundred and sixty Frenchmen and 312 Americans were killed and wounded. As the army began to retreat the British general attacked the rear, determined to annihilate the Americans. It was then that the black and mulatto freedmen from Haiti under the

---

[7] Livermore, p. 122. See also the account of Peter Salem, *do.,* pp. 118-21.

command of Viscount de Fontages made the charge on the English and saved the retreating Americans. They returned to Haiti to prepare eventually to make that country the second one in America which threw off the domination of Europe.[8]

Some idea of the number of Negro soldiers can be had by reference to documents mentioning the action of the States. Rhode Island raised a regiment of slaves, and Governor Cooke said that it was generally thought that at least 300 would enlist. Four companies were finally formed there at a cost of over £10,000. Most of the 629 slaves in New Hampshire enlisted and many of the 15,000 slaves in New York. Connecticut had Negroes in her regiments and also a regiment of coloured soldiers. Maryland sought in 1781 to raise 750 Negro troops. Massachusetts had coloured troops in her various units from 72 towns in that State. "In view of these numerous facts it is safe to conclude that there were at least 4,000 Negro soldiers scattered throughout the Continental Army."[9]

In a debate in Congress in 1820 two men, one from the North and one from the South, gave the verdict of that time on the value of the Negro in the Revolutionary War. William Eustis of Massachusetts said: "The war over and peace restored, these men returned to their respective States, and who could have said to them on their return to civil life after having shed their blood in common with the whites in the defence of the liberties of the country, 'You are not to participate in the rights secured by the struggle or in the liberty for which you have been fighting?' Certainly no white man in Massachusetts."

Charles Pinckney of South Carolina said: that the Negroes, "then were, as they still are, as valuable a part of our population to the Union as any other equal number of inhabitants. They were in numerous instances the pioneers and, in all, the labourers of your armies. To their hands were owing the erection of the greatest part of the fortifications raised for the protection of our country; some of which, particularly Fort

---

[8] T. G. Steward, in *publications American Negro Academy,* No. 5, p. 12.
[9] W. B. Hartgrove, *Journal of Negro History,* Vol. 1, pp. 125-9.

Moultrie, gave at that early period of the inexperience and untried valor of our citizens, immortality to American arms: and, in the Northern States numerous bodies of them were enrolled into and fought by the sides of the whites, the battles of the Revolution."[10]

In 1779 in the war between Spain and Great Britain, the Spanish Governor of Louisiana, Galvez, had in his army which he led against the British, numbers of blacks and mulattoes who he said "behaved on all occasions with as much valour and generosity as the whites."[11]

3. THE WAR OF 1812

In the War of 1812, the Negro appeared not only as soldier but particularly as sailor, and in the dispute concerning the impressment of American sailors which was one of the causes of the war, Negro sailors repeatedly figured as seized by England and claimed as American citizens by America for whose rights the nation was apparently ready to go to war. For instance, on the *Chesapeake* were three Negro sailors whom the British claimed but whom the Americans declared were American citizens—Ware, Martin and Strachen. As Bryant says: "The citizenship of Negroes was sought and defended by England and America at this time, but a little later it was denied by the United States Supreme Court that Negroes could be citizens." On demand two of these Negroes were returned to America by the British government; the other one died in England.

Negroes fought under Perry and Macdonough. On the high seas Negroes were fighting. Nathaniel Shaler, captain of a privateer, wrote to his agent in New York in 1813:

"Before I could get our light sails on and almost before I could turn around, I was under the guns, not of a transport but of a large frigate! And not more than a quarter of a mile from her.... Her first broadside killed two men and wounded six others.... My officers conducted themselves in a way that would have done honour to a more

---

[10] Wilson, *Black Phalanx,* p. 71.
[11] *Journal of Negro History,* Vol. 1, pp. 373-4; Gayarre's *History of Louisiana,* Vol. 3, p. 108.

permanent service.... The name of one of my poor fellows who was killed ought to be registered in the book of fame, and remembered with reverence as long as bravery is considered a virtue. He was a black man by the name of John Johnson.... When America has such tars, she has little to fear from the tyrants of the ocean."[12]

A few Negroes were in the northern armies. A Congressman said in 1828: "I myself saw a battalion of them—as fine martial looking men as I ever saw attached to the northern army in the last war (1812) on its march from Plattsburg to Sacketts Harbor where they did service for the country with credit to New York and honour to themselves."[13]

But it was in the South that they furnished the most spectacular instance of participation in this war. Governor Claiborne appealed to General Jackson to use coloured soldiers. "These men, Sir, for the most part, sustain good characters. Many of them have extensive connections and much property to defend, and all seem attached to arms. The mode of acting toward them at the present crisis, is an inquiry of importance. If we give them not our confidence, the enemy will be encouraged to intrigue and corrupt them."[14]

September 21, 1814, Jackson issued a spirited appeal to the free Negroes of Louisiana: "Through a mistaken policy, you have heretofore been deprived of a participation in the glorious struggle for national rights in which our country is engaged. This no longer shall exist.

"As sons of freedom, you are now called upon to defend our most inestimable blessing. As Americans, your country looks with confidence to her adopted children for a valorous support as a faithful return for the advantages enjoyed under her mild and equitable government. As fathers, husbands and brothers, you are summoned to rally around the standard of the Eagle, to defend all which is dear in existence.... In the sincerity of a soldier and the language of truth I address you."[15]

---

[12] Niles' *Register,* Feb. 26, 1814.
[13] Wilson, *Black Phalanx,* p. 88.
[14] Alice Dunbar-Nelson in *Journal of Negro History,* vol. 2, p. 58.
[15] Niles' Register, Vol. 7, p. 205.

He promised them the same bounty as whites and they were to have coloured non-commissioned officers. There was some attempt to have Jackson tone down this appeal and say less of "equality," but he refused to change his first draft.

The news of this proclamation created great surprise in the North but not much criticism. Indeed, things were going too badly for the Americans. The Capitol at Washington had been burned, the State of Maine was in British hands, enlistment had stopped and Northern States like New York were already arming Negroes. The Louisiana legislature, a month after Jackson's proclamation, passed an act authorizing two regiments of "men of colour" by voluntary enlistment. Slaves were allowed to enlist and were publicly manumitted for their services. There were 3,200 white and 430 coloured soldiers in the battle of New Orleans. The first battalion of 280 Negroes was commanded by a white planter, La Coste; a second battalion of 150 was raised by Captain J. B. Savary, a coloured man, from the San Dominican refugees, and commanded by Major Daquin, who was probably a quadroon.

Besides these soldiers, slaves were used in throwing up the famous cotton bale ramparts, which saved the city, and this was the idea of a black slave from Africa, who had seen the same thing done at home. Coloured men were used to reconnoitre, and the slave trader Lafitte brought a mixed band of white and black fighters to help. Curiously enough there were also Negroes on the other side, Great Britain having imported a regiment from the West Indies which was at the head of the attacking column moving against Jackson's right, together with an Irish regiment. Conceive this astounding anomaly!

The American Negro soldiers were stationed very near Jackson and his staff. Jackson himself in an address to the soldiers after the battle, complimenting the "embodied militia," said:

"To the Men of Color.—Soldiers! From the shores of Mobile I collected you to arms,—I invited you to share in the perils and to divide the glory of your white countrymen. I expected much from you; for I was not uninformed of those qualities which must render you so formidable to an invading foe. I knew that you could endure hunger and thirst and all the hardships of war. I knew that you loved the land of your nativity and that, like ourselves, you had to defend all that is most dear to man. But you surpass my hopes. I have found in you, united to these qualities, that noble enthusiasm which impels to great deeds."[16]

In the celebration of the victory which followed in the great public square, the Place d'Armes, now Jackson Square, the coloured troops shared the glory and the wounded prisoners were met by coloured nurses.[17]

4. THE [U.S.] CIVIL WAR

There were a few Negroes in the Mexican War but they went mostly as body servants to white officers and there were probably no soldiers and certainly no distinct Negro organizations. The Negro, therefore, shares little of the blood guilt of that unhallowed raid for slave soil.

At the time of the Civil War when the call came for volunteers, free Negroes everywhere offered their services to the Northern States, and everywhere their services were declined. Indeed, it was almost looked upon as insolence that they should offer to fight in this "white man's war." Not only was the war to be fought by white men but desperate effort was made to cling to the technical fact that this was a war to save the Union and not a war against slavery. Federal officials and northern army officers made effort to reassure the South that they were not abolitionists and that they were not going to touch slavery.[18]

Meantime, there began to crystallize the demand that the real object of the war be made the abolition of slavery and that the slaves and coloured men in general be allowed to fight for freedom.

This met bitter opposition. The New York *Herald* voiced this on August 5, 1862. "The efforts of those who love the Negro more than the Union to induce the President to swerve from his established policy are unavailing. He will neither be persuaded by promises nor intimidated by threats. Today he was called upon by two United States Senators and

---

[16] Niles' Register, Vol. 7, pp. 345-6.
[17] Dunbar-Nelson in *Journal of Negro History,* Vol. 2, pp. 59-60.
[18] Williams, *Negro Race in America,* Vol. 2, pp. 244 ff.

rather peremptorily requested to accept the services of two Negro regiments. They were flatly and unequivocally rejected. The President did not appreciate the necessity of employing the Negroes to fight the battles of the country and take the positions which the white men of the nation, the voters, and sons of patriotic sires, should be proud to occupy; there were employments in which the Negroes of rebel masters might well be engaged, but he was not willing to place them upon an equality with our volunteers who had left home and family and lucrative occupations to defend the Union and the Constitution while there were volunteers or militia enough in the loyal States to maintain the Government without resort to this expedient. If the loyal people were not satisfied with the policy he had adopted, he was willing to leave the administration to other hands. One of the Senators was impudent enough to tell the President he wished to God he would resign."

In the spring of 1862 General Hunter was sent into South Carolina with less than 11,000 men and charged with the duty of holding the whole seacoast of Georgia, South Carolina and Florida. He asked for re-enforcement but was told frankly from Washington, "Not a man from the North can be spared." The only way to guard the position was to keep long lines of entrenchment thrown up against the enemy. General Hunter calmly announced his intention of forming a Negro regiment to help him. They were to be paid as labourers by the quartermaster, but he expected eventually to have them recognized as soldiers by the government. At first he could find no officers. They were shocked at being asked to command "niggers." Even non-commissioned officers were difficult to find. But eventually the regiment was formed and became an object of great curiosity when on parade. Reports of the first South Carolina infantry were sent to Washington, but there was no reply. Then suddenly the matter came up in Congress and Hunter was ordered to explain whether he had enlisted fugitive slaves and upon what authority. Hunter immediately sent a sharp reply:

"To the first question, therefore, I reply: That no regiment of 'fugitive slaves' has been, or is being, organized in this department. There is, however, a fine regiment of loyal persons whose late masters are fugitive rebels—men who everywhere fly before the appearance of the National flag, leaving their loyal and unhappy servants behind them, to shift as best they can for themselves. So far, indeed, are the loyal persons composing the regiment from seeking to evade the presence of their late owners, that they are now one and all endeavouring with commendable zeal to acquire the drill and discipline requisite to place them in a position to go in full and effective pursuit of their fugacious and traitorous proprietors.

"The experiment of arming the blacks, so far as I have made it, has been a complete and even marvellous success. They are sober, docile, attentive and enthusiastic, displaying great natural capacities in acquiring the duties of the soldier. They are now eager beyond all things to take the field and be led into action; and it is the unanimous opinion of the officers who have had charge of them, that in the peculiarities of this climate and country, they will prove invaluable auxiliaries, fully equal to the similar regiments so long and so successfully used by the British authorities in the West India Islands.

"In conclusion, I would say, it is my hope—there appearing no possibility of other reinforcements, owing to the exigencies of the campaign in the peninsula—to have organized by the end of next fall and to be able to present to the government from 48,000 to 50,000 of these hardy and devoted soldiers."[19]

The reply was read in Congress amid laughter despite the indignation of the Kentucky Congressman who instituted the inquiry.

Protests now came from the South, but no answer was forthcoming, and despite all the agitation the regiment remained until at last Hunter was officially ordered to raise 50,000 black labourers of whom 5,000 might be armed and dressed as soldiers.

Horace Greeley stated the case clearly August 20, 1862 in his "Prayer of Twenty Million":[20]

---

[19] Williams, *Negro Race in America,* Vol. 2, pp. 280-82.
[20] New York *Tribune,* Aug. 19, 1862.

"On the face of this wide earth, Mr. President, there is not one disinterested, determined, intelligent champion of the Union cause who does not feel that all attempts to put down the rebellion and at the same time uphold its inciting cause are preposterous and futile—that the rebellion if crushed out tomorrow would be renewed within a year if slavery were left in full vigour—that army officers who remain to this day devoted to slavery can at best be but half-way loyal to the Union— and that every hour of deference to slavery is an hour of added and deepened peril to the Union....

"I close as I began, with the statement that what an immense majority of the loyal millions of your countrymen require of you is a frank, declared, unqualified, ungrudging execution of the laws of the land, more especially of the Confiscation Act. That Act gives freedom to the slaves of rebels coming within our lines or whom those lines may at any time enclose,—we ask you to render it due obedience by publicly requiring all your subordinates to recognize and obey it. The rebels are everywhere using the late anti-Negro riots in the North—as they have long used your officers' treatment of Negroes in the South—to convince the slaves that they have nothing to hope from a Union success—that we mean in that case to sell them into bitter bondage to defray the cost of the war. Let them impress this as a truth on the great mass of their ignorant and credulous bondsmen, and the Union will never be restored—never. We cannot conquer ten millions of people united in solid phalanx against us, powerfully aided by northern sympathizers and European allies. We must have scouts, guides, spies, cooks, teamsters, diggers and choppers from the blacks of the South—whether we allow them to fight for us or not—or we shall be baffled and repelled."

A month later, September 22, Abraham Lincoln issued the preliminary Emancipation Proclamation. He had considered this step before, and his final decision was caused, first, by a growing realization of the immense task that lay before the Union armies and, secondly, by the fear that Europe was going to recognize the Confederacy, since she saw as between North and South little difference in attitude toward slavery.

The effect of the step was undoubtedly decisive for ultimate victory, although at first it spread dismay. Six of the Northern States went Democratic in the fall elections and elsewhere the Republicans lost heavily. In the army some officers resigned and others threatened to because "The war for the Union was changed into a war for the Negro."

In the South men like Beauregard urged the raising of the "Black Flag" while Jefferson Davis in his third annual message wrote: "We may well leave it to the instincts of that common humanity which a beneficent Creator has implanted in the breasts of our fellowmen of all countries to pass judgment on a measure by which several millions of human beings of an inferior race, peaceful and contented labourers in their sphere, are doomed to extermination."[21]

With emancipation foreshadowed the full recognition of the Negro soldier was inevitable. In September 1862 came a black Infantry Regiment from Louisiana and later a regiment of heavy artillery and by the end of 1862 four Negro regiments had enlisted. Immediately after the signing of the Emancipation Proclamation came the Kansas Coloured volunteers and the famous 54th Massachusetts Regiment. A Bureau was established in Washington to handle the coloured enlistments and before the end of the war 178,975 Negroes had enlisted.

"In the [War] Department the actual number of Negroes enlisted was never known, from the fact that a practice prevailed of putting a live Negro in a dead one's place. For instance, if a company on picket or scouting lost ten men, the officer would immediately put ten new men in their places and have them answer to the dead men's names. I learn from very reliable sources that this was done in Virginia, also in Missouri and Tennessee. If the exact number of men could be ascertained, instead of 180,000 it would doubtless be in the neighbourhood of 220,000 who entered the ranks of the army."[22]

General orders covering the enlistment of Negro troops were sent out from the War Department October 13, 1863. The Union League

---

[21] Williams, Vol. 2, p. 271.
[22] Wilson, p. 123.

in New York city raised 2,000 black soldiers in 45 days, although no bounty was offered them and no protection promised their families. The regiment had a triumphal march through the city and a daily paper stated: "In the month of July last the homes of these people were burned and pillaged by an infuriated political mob; they and their families were hunted down and murdered in the public streets of this city; and the force and majesty of the law were powerless to protect them. Seven brief months have passed and a thousand of these despised and persecuted men marched through the city in the garb of the United States soldiers, in vindication of their own manhood and with the approval of a countless multitude—in effect saving from inevitable and distasteful conscription the same number of those who hunted their persons and destroyed their homes during those days of humiliation and disgrace. This is noble vengeance—a vengeance taught by Him who commanded, 'Love them that hate you; do good to them that persecute you.'"

The enlistment of Negroes caused difficulty and friction among the white troops. In South Carolina General Gilmore had to forbid the white troops using Negro troops for menial service in cleaning up the camps. Black soldiers in uniform often had their uniforms stripped off by white soldiers.

"I attempted to pass Jackson Square in New Orleans one day in my uniform when I was met by two white soldiers of the 24th Conn. They halted me and then ordered me to undress. I refused, when they seized me and began to tear my coat off. I resisted, but to no good purpose; a half dozen others came up and began to assist. I recognized a sergeant in the crowd, an old shipmate on board of a New Bedford, Mass., whaler; he came to my rescue, my clothing was restored and I was let go. It was nothing strange to see a black soldier *à la* Adam come into the barracks out of the streets."[23] This conduct led to the killing of a portion of a boat's crew of the U. S. Gunboat *Jackson*, at Ship Island, Miss., by members of a Negro regiment stationed there.

---

[23] Wilson, p. 132.

Then, too, there was contemptible discrimination in pay. While white soldiers received $13 a month and clothing, Negro soldiers, by act of Congress, were given $10 a month with $3 deducted for clothing, leaving only $7 a month as actual pay. This was only remedied when the 54th Massachusetts Infantry refused all pay for a year until it should be treated as other regiments. The State of Massachusetts made up the difference between the $7 and $13 to disabled soldiers until June 16, 1864, when the government finally made the Negroes' pay equal to that of the whites.

On the Confederate side there was a movement to use Negro soldiers fostered by Judah Benjamin, General Lee and others. In 1861 a Negro company from Nashville offered its services to the Confederate states and free Negroes of Memphis were authorized by the Committee of Safety to organize a volunteer company. Companies of free Negroes were raised in New Orleans,—"Very well drilled and comfortably uniformed." In Richmond, coloured troops were also raised in the last days. Few if any of these saw actual service. Plantation hands from Alabama built the redoubts at Charleston, and Negroes worked as teamsters and helpers throughout the South. In February 1864, the Confederate congress provided for the impressment of 20,000 slaves for menial service, and President Davis suggested that the number be doubled and that they be emancipated at the end of their service. Before the war started local authorities had in many cases enrolled free Negroes as soldiers and some of these remained in the service of the Confederacy. The adjutant general of the Louisiana militia issued an order which said "the Governor and the Commander-in-Chief, relying implicitly upon the loyalty of the free coloured population of the city and State, for the protection of their homes, their property and for southern rights, from the population of a ruthless invader, and believing that the military organization which existed prior to February 15, 1862, and elicited praise and respect for the patriotic motives which prompted it, should exist for and during the war, calls upon them to maintain their organization and hold themselves prepared for such orders as may be transmitted to them." These native guards did not leave the city when the Confederates did and explained to General Butler that they dared not refuse to work with the Confederates and that they hoped by their service to gain greater equality with the whites and that they would be glad now to join the Union forces. Two weeks after the fall of Sumter coloured volunteers passed through Georgia on their way to Virginia. There were 16 or more companies. In November, 1861, a regiment of 1,400 free coloured men were in the line of march at New Orleans. The idea of calling the Negroes grew as the power of the Confederacy waned and the idea of emancipation as compensation spread. President Davis said "Should the alternative ever be presented of subjugation or of the employment of slaves as soldiers there seems no reason to doubt what should be our decision."

There was, of course, much difference of opinion. General Cobb said "If slaves make good soldiers our whole theory of slavery is wrong," while a Georgian replied "Some say that Negroes will not fight, I say they will fight. They fought at Ocean Pond, Honey Hill and other places." General Lee, in January '64, gave as his opinion that they should employ them without delay. "I believe with proper regulations they may be made efficient soldiers." He continued, "Our chief aim should be to secure their fidelity. There have been formidable armies composed of men having no interest in the cause for which they fought beyond their pay or the hope of plunder. But it is certain that the surest foundation upon which the fidelity of an army can rest, especially in a service which imposes hardships and privations, is the personal interest of the soldier in the issue of the contest. Such an interest we can give our Negroes by giving immediate freedom to all who enlist, and freedom at the end of the war to the families of those who discharge their duties faithfully (whether they survive or not), together with the privilege of residing at the South. To this might be added a bounty for faithful service."

Finally, March 13, 1865, it was directed that slaves be enrolled in the Confederate army, each state to furnish its quota of 300,000.

Recruiting officers were appointed, but before the plan could be carried out, Lee and Johnson surrendered.[24]

The central fact which we forget in these days is that the real question in the minds of most white people in the United States in 1863 was whether or not the Negro really would fight. The generation then living had never heard of the Negro in the Revolution and in the War of 1812, much less of his struggles and insurrections before. From 1820 down to the time of the war a determined and far-reaching propaganda had led most men to believe in the natural inferiority, cowardice and degradation of the Negro race. We have already seen Abraham Lincoln suggest that if arms were put into the hands of the Negro soldier it might be simply a method of arming the rebels. The New York *Times* discussed the matter soberly, defending the right to employ Negroes but suggesting four grounds which might make it inexpedient; that Negroes would not fight, that prejudice was so strong that whites would not fight with them, that no free Negroes would volunteer and that slaves could not be gotten hold of and that the use of Negroes would exasperate the South. "The very best thing that can be done under existing circumstances, in our judgment, is to possess our souls in patience while the experiment is being tried. The problem will probably speedily solve itself—much more speedily than heated discussion or harsh criminations can solve it."

This was in February 16, 1863. It was not long before the results of using Negro troops began to be reported and we find the *Times* saying editorially on the 31st of July: "Negro soldiers have now been in battle at Port Hudson and at Milliken's Bend in Louisiana; at Helena in Arkansas, at Morris Island in South Carolina, and at or near Fort Gibson in the Indian Territory. In two of these instances they assaulted fortified positions and led the assault; in two they fought on the defensive, and in one they attacked rebel infantry. In all of them they acted in conjunction with white troops and under command of white officers. In some instances they acted with distinguished bravery, and in all they acted as well as could be expected of raw troops."

---

[24] Wesley, in *Journal of Negro History,* Vol. 4, pp. 239 ff.

On the 11th of February, 1863, the news columns of the *Times* were still more enthusiastic. "It will not need many such reports as this— and there have been several before it—to shake our inveterate Saxon prejudice against the capacity and courage of Negro troops. Everybody knows that they were used in the Revolution, and in the last war with Great Britain fought side by side with white troops, and won equal praises from Washington and Jackson. It is shown also that black sailors are on equal terms with their white comrades. If on the sea, why not on the land? No officer who has commanded black troops has yet reported against them. They are tried in the most unfavourable and difficult circumstances, but never fail. When shall we learn to use the full strength of the formidable ally who is only waiting for a summons to rally under the flag of the Union? Colonel Higginson says: 'No officer in this regiment now doubts that the successful prosecution of this war lies in the unlimited employment of black troops.' The remark is true in a military sense, and it has a still deeper political significance.

"When General Hunter has scattered 50,000 muskets among the Negroes of the Carolinas, and General Butler has organized the 100,000 or 200,000 blacks for whom he may perhaps shortly carry arms to New Orleans, the possibility of restoring the Union as it was, with slavery again its dormant power, will be seen to have finally passed away. The Negro is indeed the key to success."

The Negroes began to fight and fight hard; but their own and peculiar characteristics stood out even in the blood of war. A Pennsylvania Major wrote home: "I find that these coloured men learn everything that pertains to the duties of a soldier much faster than any white soldiers I have ever seen.... They are willing, obedient, and cheerful; move with agility, and are full of music."[25]

Certain battles, carnivals of blood, stand out and despite their horror must not be forgotten. One of the earliest encounters was the terrible massacre at Fort Pillow, April 18, 1863. The fort was held with a garrison of 557 men, of whom 262 were coloured soldiers of the 6th

---

[25] New York *Tribune,* Nov. 14, 1863; Williams, Vol. 2, p. 347.

United States Heavy Artillery. The Union commander refused to surrender.

"Upon receiving the refusal of Major Booth to capitulate, Forrest gave a signal and his troops made a frantic charge upon the fort. It was received gallantly and resisted stubbornly, but there was no use of fighting. In ten minutes the enemy, assaulting the fort in the centre, and striking it on the flanks, swept in. The Federal troops surrendered; but an indiscriminate massacre followed. Men were shot down in their tracks; pinioned to the ground with bayonet and sabre. Some were clubbed to death while dying of wounds; others were made to get down upon their knees, in which condition they were shot to death. Some were burned alive, having been fastened into the buildings, while still others were nailed against the houses, tortured and then burned to a crisp."[26]

May 27, 1863, came the battle of Port Hudson. "Hearing the firing apparently more fierce and continuous to the right than anywhere else, I turned in that direction, past the sugar house of Colonel Chambers, where I had slept, and advanced to near the pontoon bridge across the Big Sandy Bayou, which the Negro regiments had erected, and where they were fighting most desperately. I had seen these brave and hitherto despised fellows the day before as I rode along the lines, and I had seen General Banks acknowledge their respectful salute as he would have done that of any white troops; but still the question was—with too many—Will they fight?'

"General Dwight, at least, must have had the idea, not only that they were men, but something more than men, from the terrific test to which he put their valour. Before any impression had been made upon the earthworks of the enemy, and in full face of the batteries belching forth their 62-pounders, these devoted people rushed forward to encounter grape, canister, shell, and musketry, with no artillery but two small howitzers—that seemed mere popguns to their adversaries—and no reserve whatever.

---

[26] Williams, Vol. 2, p. 360.

THE NEED FOR HEROES

"Their force consisted of the 1st Louisiana Native Guards (with coloured field officers) under Lieutenant-Colonel Bassett, and the 3d Louisiana Native Guards, Colonel Nelson (with white field officers), the whole under command of the latter officer.

"On going into action they were 1,080 strong, and formed into four lines, Lieutenant-Colonel Bassett, 1st Louisiana, forming the first line, and Lieutenant-Colonel Henry Finnegas the second. When ordered to charge up the works, they did so with the skill and nerve of old veterans (black people, be it remembered who had never been in action before). Oh, but the fire from the rebel guns was so terrible upon the unprotected masses, that the first few shots mowed them down like grass and so continued.

"Colonel Bassett being driven back, Colonel Finnegas took his place, and his men being similarly cut to pieces, Lieutenant-Colonel Bassett reformed and recommenced; and thus these brave people went in from morning until 3:30 PM, under the most hideous carnage that men ever had to withstand, and that very few white ones would have had nerve to encounter, even if ordered to.

"During this time, they rallied, and were ordered to make six distinct charges, losing 37 killed, and 155 wounded, and 116 missing,— the majority, if not all, of these being, in all probability, now lying dead on the gory field, and without the rites of sepulture; for when, by flag of truce, our forces in other directions were permitted to reclaim their dead, the benefit, through some neglect, was not extended to these black regiments.

"The deeds of heroism performed by these coloured men were such as the proudest white men might emulate. Their colours are torn to pieces by shot and literally bespattered by blood and brains. The colour-sergeant of the 1st Louisiana, on being mortally wounded, hugged the colours to his breast, when a struggle ensued between the two colour-corporals on each side of him, as to who should have the honour of bearing the sacred standard, and during this generous contention one was seriously wounded. One black lieutenant actually mounted the enemy's works three or four times, and in one charge the assaulting party came within fifty paces of them. Indeed, if only ordinarily supported by artillery and reserve, no one can convince us that they would not have opened a passage through the enemy's works.

"Captain Callioux of the 1st Louisiana, a man so black that he actually prided himself upon his blackness, died the death of a hero, leading on his men in the thickest of the fight."[27]

In July 13, 1863, came the draft riot in New York when the daily papers told the people that they were called upon to fight the battles of "niggers and abolitionists," when the governor did nothing but "request" the rioters to await the report of his demand that the President suspend the draft. Meantime the city was given over to rapine and murder, property destroyed, Negroes killed and the coloured orphans' asylum burned to the ground and property robbed and pillaged.

At that very time, in South Carolina, black soldiers were preparing to take Fort Wagner, their greatest battle. It will be noted that continually Negroes were called upon to rescue lost causes, many times as a sort of deliberate test of their courage. Fort Wagner was a case in point. The story may be told from two points of view, that of the white Unionist and that of the Confederate. The Union account says:

"The signal given, our forces advanced rapidly towards the fort, while our mortars in the rear tossed their bombs over their heads. The 54th Massachusetts (a Negro Regiment) led the attack, supported by the 6th Connecticut, 48th New York, 3rd New Hampshire, 76th Pennsylvania, and the 9th Maine Regiments.... The silent and shattered walls of Wagner all at once burst forth into a blinding sheet of vivid light, as though they had suddenly been transformed by some magic power into the living, seething crater of a volcano! Down came the whirlwind of destruction along the beach with the swiftness of lightning! How fearfully the hissing shot, the shrieking bombs, the whistling bars of iron, and the whispering bullet struck and crushed through the dense masses of our brave men! I never shall forget the terrible sound of that awful blast of death, which swept down, shattered or dead, a thousand of our

---

[27] New York *Times,* June 13, 1863.

men. Not a shot had missed its aim. Every bolt of steel, every globe of iron and lead, tasted of human blood....

"In a moment the column recovered itself, like a gallant ship at sea when buried for an instant under the immense wave.

"The ditch is reached; a thousand men leap into it, clamber up the shattered ramparts, and grapple with the foe, which yields and falls back to the rear of the fort. Our men swarm over the walls, bayoneting the desperate rebel cannoneers. Hurrah! the fort is ours!

"But now came another blinding blast from concealed guns in the rear of the fort, and our men went down by scores.... The struggle is terrific. Our supports hurry up to the aid of their comrades, but as they reach the ramparts they fire a volley which strikes down many of our men. Fatal mistake! Our men rally once more; but, in spite of an heroic resistance, they are forced back again to the edge of the ditch. Here the brave Shaw, with scores of his black warriors, went down, fighting desperately."

When asking for the body of Colonel Shaw, a confederate major said: "We have buried him with his niggers."

The Confederate account is equally eloquent.

"The carnage was frightful. It is believed the Federals lost more men on that eventful night than twice the entire strength of the Confederate garrison.... According to the statement of Chaplain Dennison the assaulting columns, in two brigades, commanded by General Strong and Colonel Putnam (the division under General Seymour), consisted of the 54th Massachusetts, 3rd and 7th New Hampshire, 6th Connecticut and 100th New York, with a reserve brigade commanded by General Stephenson. One of the assaulting regiments was composed of Negroes (the 54th Massachusetts) and to it was assigned the honour of leading the white columns to the charge. It was a dearly purchased compliment. Their Colonel (Shaw) was killed upon the parapet and the regiment almost annihilated, although the

Confederates in the darkness could not tell the colour of their assailants."[28]

At last it was seen that Negro troops could do more than useless or helpless or impossible tasks, and in the siege of Petersburg they were put to important work. When the general attack was ordered on the 16th of June, 1864, a division of black troops was used. The Secretary of War, Stanton himself, saw them and said:

"The hardest fighting was done by the black troops. The forts they stormed were the worst of all. After the affair was over General Smith went to thank them, and tell them he was proud of their courage and dash. He says they cannot be exceeded as soldiers, and that hereafter he will send them in a difficult place as readily as the best white troops."[29]

It was planned to send the coloured troops under Burnside against the enemy after the great mine was exploded. Inspecting officers reported to Burnside that the black division was fitted for this perilous work. The white division which was sent made a fiasco of it. Then, after all had been lost Burnside was ready to send in his black division and though they charged again and again they were repulsed and the Union lost over 4,000 men killed, wounded and captured.

All the officers of the coloured troops in the Civil War were not white. From the first there were many coloured non-commissioned officers, and the Louisiana regiments raised under Butler had 66 coloured officers, including one Major and 27 Captains, besides the full quota of non-commissioned coloured officers. In the Massachusetts coloured troops there were 10 commissioned Negro officers and 3 among the Kansas troop. Among these officers was a Lieutenant-Colonel Reed of North Carolina, who was killed in battle. In Kansas there was Captain H. F. Douglas, and in other United States' volunteer regiments were Major M. H. Delaney and Captain O. S. B. Wall; Dr. A. T. Augusta, surgeon, was brevetted Lieutenant-Colonel. The losses of

---

[28] Wilson, pp. 250-54.
[29] Williams, Vol. 2, p. 338.

Negro troops in the Civil War, killed, wounded and missing has been placed at 68,178.

Such was the service of the Negro in the Civil War. Men say that the nation gave them freedom, but the verdict of history is written on the Shaw monument at the head of Boston Common:

THE WHITE OFFICERS

Taking Life and Honor in their Hands—Cast their lot with Men of a Despised Race Unproved in War—and Risked Death as Inciters of a Servile Insurrection if Taken Prisoners, Besides Encountering all the Common Perils of Camp, March, and Battle.

THE BLACK RANK AND FILE

Volunteered when Disaster Clouded the Union Cause—Served without Pay for Eighteen Months till Given that of White Troops— Faced Threatened Enslavement if Captured—Were Brave in Action— Patient under Dangerous and Heavy Labors and Cheerful amid Hardships and Privations.

TOGETHER

They Gave to the Nation Undying Proof that Americans of African Descent Possess the Pride, Courage, and Devotion of the Patriot Soldier—One Hundred and Eighty Thousand Such Americans Enlisted Under the Union Flag in MDCCCLXIII-MDCCCLXV.

5. THE WAR IN CUBA

In the Spanish-American War four Negro regiments were among the first to be ordered to the front. They were the regular army regiments, 24th and 25th Infantry, and the 9th and 10th Cavalry. President McKinley recommended that new regiments of regular army troops be formed among Negroes but Congress took no action. Coloured troops with coloured officers were formed as follows: The 3rd North Carolina, the 8th Illinois, the 9th Battalion, Ohio and the 23rd Kansas. Regiments known as the Immunes, being immune to Yellow fever, were formed with coloured lieutenants and white captains and field officers, and called the 7th, 8th, 9th and 10th United States Volunteers. In addition to those there were the 6th Virginia with coloured lieutenants and the 3rd Alabama with white officers. Indiana had two companies attached to the 8th Immunes. None of the Negro volunteer companies reached the front in time to take part in battle. The 8th Illinois formed a part of the Army of Occupation and was noted for its policing and cleaning up of Santiago. Colonel John R. Marshall, commanding the 8th Illinois, and Major Charles Young, a regular army commander, both coloured, were in charge of the battalion.

The coloured regular army regiments took a brilliant part in the war. The first regiment ordered to the front was the 24th Infantry. Negro soldiers were in the battles around Santiago. The Tenth Cavalry made an effective attack at Las Quasimas and at El Caney on July 1 they saved Roosevelt's Rough Riders from annihilation. The 24th Infantry volunteered in the Yellow fever epidemic and cleaned the camp in one day. *Review of Reviews* says: "One of the most gratifying incidents of the Spanish War has been the enthusiasm that the coloured regiments of the regular army have aroused throughout the whole country. Their fighting at Santiago was magnificent. The Negro soldiers showed excellent discipline, the highest qualities of personal bravery, very superior physical endurance, unfailing good temper, and the most generous disposition toward all comrades-in-arms, whether white or black. Roosevelt's Rough Riders have come back singing the praises of the coloured troops. There is not a dissenting voice in the chorus of praise.... Men who can fight for their country as did these coloured troops ought to have their full share of gratitude and honour."

6. CARRIZAL

In 1916, the United States sent a punitive expedition under General Pershing into Mexico in pursuit of the Villa forces which had raided Columbus, New Mexico. Two Negro regiments, the 10th Cavalry and the 24th Infantry, were a part of his expedition. On June 21, Troop C and K of the 10th Cavalry were ambushed at Carrizal by some 700 Mexican soldiers. Although outnumbered almost ten to one, these black soldiers dismounted in the face of a withering machine-gun fire, deployed, charged the Mexicans and killed their commander.

This handful of men fought on until, of the three officers commanding them, two were killed and one was badly wounded. Seventeen of the men were killed and twenty-three were made prisoners. One of the many outstanding heroes of this memorable engagement was Peter Bigstaff, who fought to the last beside his commander, Lieutenant Adair. A Southern white man, with no love for blacks, wrote:

"The black trooper might have faltered and fled a dozen times, saving his own life and leaving Adair to fight alone. But it never seemed to occur to him. He was a comrade to the last blow. When Adair's broken revolver fell from his hand the black trooper pressed another into it, and together, shouting in defiance, they thinned the swooping circle of overwhelming odds before them.

"The black man fought in the deadly shambles side by side with the white man, following always, fighting always as his lieutenant fought.

"And finally, when Adair, literally shot to pieces, fell in his tracks, his last command to his black trooper was to leave him and save his life. Even then the heroic Negro paused in the midst of that Hell of carnage for a final service to his officer. Bearing a charmed life, he had fought his way out. He saw that Adair had fallen with his head in the water. With superb loyalty the black trooper turned and went back to the maelstrom of death, lifted the head of his superior, leaned him against a tree and left him there dead with dignity when it was impossible to serve any more.

"There is not a finer piece of soldierly devotion and heroic comradeship in the history of modern warfare than that of Henry Adair and the black trooper who fought by him at Carrizal."[30]

7. THE [FIRST] WORLD WAR

Finally we come to the World War the history of which is not yet written. At first and until the United States entered the war the Negro figured as

---

[30] John Temple Graves in *Review of Reviews*.

a labourer and a great exodus took place from the South as we have already noted. Some effort was made to keep the Negro from the draft but finally he was called and although constituting less than a tenth of the population he furnished 13 percent of the soldiers called to the colours. The registry for the draft had insulting colour discriminations and determined effort was made to confine Negroes to stevedore and labour regiments under white officers. Most of the Negro draftees were thus sent to the Service of Supplies where they were largely under illiterate whites and suffered greatly. Finally, a camp for training Negro officers was established and nearly 700 Negroes commissioned, none of them, however, above the rank of captain; Charles Young, the highest ranking Negro graduate of West Point and one of the best officers in the army was kept from the front, because being already a colonel with a distinguished record he would surely have become a general if sent to France.

Two Negro divisions were planned, the 92nd and the 93rd. The 93rd was to be composed of the Negro National Guard regiments all of whom had some and one all Negro officers. The latter division was never organized as a complete division but four of its regiments were sent to France and encountered bitter discrimination from the Americans on account of their Negro officers. They were eventually brigaded with the French and saw some of the hardest fighting of the war in the final drive toward Sedan. They were cited in General Orders as follows by General Goybet:[31]

"In transmitting to you with legitimate pride the thanks and congratulations of the General Garnier Duplessis, allow me, my dear friends of all ranks, Americans and French, to thank you from the bottom of my heart as a chief and a soldier for the expression of gratitude for the glory which you have lent our good 157th Division. I had full confidence in you but you have surpassed my hopes.

"During these nine days of hard fighting you have progressed nine kilometres through powerful organized defences, taken nearly 600

---

[31] MS. Copies of Orders.

THE NEED FOR HEROES

prisoners, 15 guns of different calibres, 20 minnewerfers [sic],[32] and nearly 150 machine guns, secured an enormous amount of engineering material, an important supply of artillery ammunition, brought down by your fire three enemy aeroplanes.

"Your troops have been admirable in their attack. You must be proud of the courage of your officers and men; and I consider it an honour to have them under my command.

"The bravery and dash of your regiment won the admiration of the 2nd Moroccan Division who are themselves versed in warfare. Thanks to you, during those hard days, the Division was at all times in advance of all other divisions of the Army Corps. I am sending you all my thanks and beg you to transmit them to your subordinates.

"I called on your wounded. Their morale is higher than any praise.

GOYBET."

The 92nd Division encountered difficulties in organization and was never assembled as a Division until it arrived in France. There it was finally gotten in shape and took a small part in the Argonne offensive and in the fight just preceding the armistice. Their Commanding General said:[33]

"Five months ago today the 92nd Division landed in France.

"After seven weeks of training, it took over a sector in the front line, and since that time some portion of the Division has been practically continuously under fire.

"It participated in the last battle of the war with creditable success, continuously pressing the attack against highly organized defensive works. It advanced successfully on the first day of the battle, attaining its objectives and capturing prisoners. This in the face of determined opposition by an alert enemy, and against rifle, machine-gun and artillery fire. The issue of the second day's battle was rendered

---

[32] Minenwerfers were light mortars extensively used by the German artillery in World War I –Ed.
[33] MS. Copies of orders.

indecisive by the order to cease firing at eleven A.M.—when the armistice became effective."

With the small chance thus afforded Negro troops nevertheless made a splendid record and especially those under Negro officers. If they had had larger opportunity and less organized prejudice they would have done much more. Perhaps their greatest credit is from the fact that they withstood so bravely and uncomplainingly the barrage of hatred and offensive prejudice aimed against them. The young Negro officers especially made a splendid record as to thinking, guiding leaders of an oppressed group.

Thus has the black man defended America from the beginning to the World War. To him our independence from Europe and slavery is in no small degree due.

CHAPTER IV
The Emancipation of Democracy

How the black slave by his incessant struggle to be free has broadened the basis of democracy in America and in the world.

Help in exploration, labour unskilled and to some extent skilled, and fighting, have been the three gifts which so far we have considered as having been contributed by black folk to America. We now turn to a matter more indefinite and yet perhaps of greater importance.

Without the active participation of the Negro in the Civil War, the Union could not have been saved nor slavery destroyed in the nineteenth century.[34] Without the help of black soldiers, the independence of the United States could not have been gained in the eighteenth century. But the Negro's contribution to America was at once

---

[34] At least this was the opinion of Abraham Lincoln—cf. Wilson's *Black Phalanx*, p. 108.

more subtle and important than these things. Dramatically the Negro is the central thread of American history. The whole story turns on him whether we think of the dark and flying slave ship in the sixteenth century, the expanding plantations of the seventeenth, the swelling commerce of the eighteenth, or the fight for freedom in the nineteenth. It was the black man that raised a vision of democracy in America such as neither Americans nor Europeans conceived in the eighteenth century and such as they have not even accepted in the twentieth century; and yet a conception which every clear sighted man knows is true and inevitable.

1. DEMOCRACY

Democracy was not planted full grown in America. It was a slow growth beginning in Europe and developing further and more quickly in America. It did not envisage at first the man farthest down as a participant in democratic privilege or even as a possible participant. This was not simply because of the inability of the ignorant and degraded to express themselves and act intelligently and efficiently, but it was a failure to recognize that the mass of men had any rights which the better class were bound to respect. Thus democracy to the world first meant simply the transfer of privilege and opportunity from waning to waxing power, from the well-born to the rich, from the nobility to the merchants. Divine Right of birth yielded the Divine Right of wealth. Growing industry, business and commerce were putting economic and social power into the hands of what we call the middle class. Political opportunity to correspond with this power was the demand of the eighteenth century and this was what the eighteenth century called Democracy. On the other hand, both in Europe and in America, there were classes, and large classes, without power and without consideration whose place in democracy was inconceivable both to Europeans and Americans. Among these were the agricultural serfs and industrial labourers of Europe and the indentured servants and black slaves of America. The white serfs, as they were transplanted in America, began a slow, but in the end, effective agitation for recognition in American democracy. And through them has risen the modern American labour movement. But this movement almost from the first looked for its triumph along the ancient paths of aristocracy and sought to raise the white servant and labourer on the backs of the black servant and slave. If now the black man had been inert, unintelligent, submissive, democracy would have continued to mean in America what it means so widely still in Europe, the admission of the powerful to participation in government and privilege in so far and only in so far as their power becomes irresistible. It would not have meant a recognition of human beings as such and the giving of economic and social power to the powerless.

It is usually assumed in reading American history that whatever the Negro has done for America has been passive and unintelligent, that he accompanied the explorers as a beast of burden and accomplished whatever he did by sheer accident; that he laboured because he was driven to labour and fought because he was made to fight. This is not true. On the contrary, it was the rise and growth among the slaves of a determination to be free and an active part of American democracy that forced American democracy continually to look into the depths; that held the faces of American thought to the inescapable fact that as long as there was a slave in America, America could not be a free republic; and more than that: as long as there were people in America, slave or nominally free, who could not participate in government and industry and society as free, intelligent human beings, our democracy had failed of its greatest mission.

This great vision of the black man was, of course, at first the vision of the few, as visions always are, but it was always there; it grew continuously and it developed quickly from wish to active determination. One cannot think then of democracy in America or in the modern world without reference to the American Negro. The democracy established in America in the eighteenth century was not, and was not designed to be, a democracy of the masses of men and it was thus singularly easy for people to fail to see the incongruity of democracy and slavery. It was the Negro himself who forced the consideration of this incongruity, who made emancipation inevitable and made the modern world at least consider if not wholly accept the idea of a democracy including men of all races and colours.

2. INFLUENCE ON WHITE THOUGHT

Naturally, at first, it was the passive presence of the Negro with his pitiable suffering and sporadic expression of unrest that bothered the American colonists. Massachusetts and Connecticut early in the seventeenth century tried to compromise with their consciences by declaring that there should be no slavery except of persons "willingly selling themselves" or "sold to us." And these were to have "All the liberties and Christian usages which the law of God established in Israel." Massachusetts even took a strong stand against proven "man stealing"; but it was left to a little band of Germans in Pennsylvania, in 1688, to make the first clear statement the moment they looked upon a black slave: "Now, though they are black, we cannot conceive there is more liberty to have them slaves than it is to have other white ones. There is a saying that we shall do to all men like as we will be done to ourselves, making no difference of what generation, descent or colour they are. Here is liberty of conscience which is right and reasonable. Here ought also to be liberty of the body."[35]

In the eighteenth century, Sewall of Massachusetts attacked slavery. From that time down until 1863 man after man and prophet after prophet spoke against slavery and they spoke not so much as theorists but as people facing extremely uncomfortable facts. Oglethorpe would keep slavery out of Georgia because he saw how the strength of South Carolina went to defending themselves against possible slave insurrection rather than to defending the English colonies against the Spanish. The matter of baptizing the heathen whom slavery was supposed to convert brought tremendous heart searchings and argument and disputations and explanatory laws throughout the colonies. Contradictory benevolences were evident as when the Society

---

[35] Thomas, *Attitude of Friends toward Slavery,* p. 267 and Appendix.

for the Propagation of the Gospel sought to convert the Negroes and American legislatures sought to make the perpetual slavery of the converts sure.

The religious conscience, especially as it began to look upon America as a place of freedom and refuge, was torn by the presence of slavery. Late in the eighteenth and early in the nineteenth centuries pressure began to be felt from the more theoretical philanthropists of Europe and the position of American philanthropists was made correspondingly uncomfortable. Benjamin Franklin pointed out some of the evils of slavery; James Otis inveighing against England's economic tyranny acknowledged the rights of black men. Patrick Henry said that slavery was "repugnant to the first impression of right and wrong" and George Washington hoped slavery might be abolished. Thomas Jefferson made the celebrated statement: "Indeed I tremble for my country when I reflect that God is just; that His justice cannot sleep forever; that considering numbers, nature, and natural means only, a revolution of the wheel of fortune, an exchange of situation, is among possible events; that it may become probable by supernatural interference! The Almighty has no attribute which can take side with us in such a contest."[36]

Henry Laurens said to his son: "You know, my dear son, I abhor slavery. I was born in a country where slavery had been established by British kings and parliaments, as well as by the laws of that country ages before my existence. I found the Christian religion and slavery growing under the same authority and cultivation. I nevertheless disliked it. In former days there was no combating the prejudices of men supported by interest; the day I hope is approaching when, from principles of gratitude as well as justice, every man will strive to be foremost in showing his readiness to comply with the golden rule."[37]

---

[36] Jefferson's Writings, Vol. 8, pp. 403-4.
[37] George Liveermore, *Opinions of the Founders of the Republic on Negroes as Slaves, as Citizens, and as Soldiers,* Boston, 1862, p. 61.

THE NEED FOR HEROES

The first draft of the Declaration of Independence harangued King George III of Britain for the presence of slavery in the United States:

"He has waged cruel war against human nature itself, violating its most sacred rights of life and liberty in the persons of a distant people who never offended him; captivating and carrying them into slavery in another hemisphere, or to incur miserable death in their transportation thither. This piratical warfare, the opprobrium of Infidel powers, is the warfare of the Christian king of Great Britain. Determined to keep open market where men should be bought and sold, he has prostituted his negative for suppressing every legislative attempt to prohibit or to restrain this execrable commerce. And, that this assemblage of horrors might want no fact of distinguished die, he is now exciting those very people to rise in arms among us, and to purchase that liberty of which he has deprived them, by murdering the people on whom we also obtruded them; thus paying off former crimes committed against the liberties of one people with crimes which he urges them to commit against the lives of another."[38]

The final draft of the Declaration said: "We hold these truths to be self-evident:—that all men are created equal, that they are endowed by their Creator with certain inalienable rights; that among these are life, liberty, and the pursuit of happiness. That to secure these rights, governments are instituted among men, deriving their just powers from the consent of the governed."

It was afterward argued that Negroes were not included in this general statement and Judge Taney in his celebrated decision said in 1857:

They had for more than a century before been regarded as beings of an inferior order, and altogether unfit to associate with the white race, either in social or political relations; and so far inferior that they had no rights which the white man was bound to

---

[38] Jefferson's Works, Vol. 1, pp. 23-4.

respect; and that the Negro might justly and lawfully be reduced to slavery for his benefit....[39]

This *obiter dictum* was disputed by equally learned justices. Justice McLean said in his opinion:

> Our independence was a great epoch in the history of freedom; and while I admit the Government was not made especially for the coloured race, yet many of them were citizens of the New England States, and exercised the rights of suffrage when the Constitution was adopted; and it was not doubted by any intelligent person that its tendencies would greatly ameliorate their condition.[40]

Justice Curtis also said:

> It has been often asserted, that the Constitution was made exclusively by and for the white race. It has already been shown that in five of the thirteen original States, coloured persons then possessed the elective franchise and were among those by whom the Constitution was ordained and established. If so, it is not true, in point of fact, that the Constitution was made exclusively by the white race. And that it was made exclusively for the white race is, in my opinion, not only an assumption not warranted by anything in the Constitution, but contradicted by its opening declaration, that it was ordained and established by the people of the United States, for themselves and their posterity. And, as free coloured persons were then citizens of at least five States, they were among those for whom and whose posterity the Constitution was ordained and established.[41]

After the Revolution came the series of State acts abolishing slavery, beginning with Vermont in 1777; and then came the pause and retrogression followed by the slow but determined rise of the Cotton

---

[39] Howard's reports, Vol. 19.
[40] Howard's reports,, pp. 536-8.
[41] Howard's Reports, pp. 572-3, 582.

Kingdom. But even in that day the prophets protested. Hezekiah Niles said in 1819: "We are ashamed of the thing we practice; ... there is no attribute of Heaven that takes part with us, and we know it. And in the contest that must come, and will come, there will be a heap of sorrows such as the world has rarely seen."[42] While the wild preacher, Lorenzo Dow, raised his cry from the wilderness even in Alabama and Mississippi, saying: "In the rest of the Southern States the influence of these Foreigners will be known and felt in its time, and the seeds from the HORY ALLIANCE and the DECAPIGANDI, who have a hand in those grades of Generals, from the Inquisitor to the Vicar General and down.... The STRUGGLE will be DREADFUL! The CUP will be BITTER! and when the agony is over, those who survive may see better days! FAREWELL!"[43] Finally came William Lloyd Garrison and John Brown.

3. INSURRECTION

It may be said, and it usually has been said, that all this showed the natural conscience and humanity of white Americans protesting and eventually triumphing over political and economic temptations. But to this must be added the inescapable fact that the attitude, thought and action of the Negro himself was in the largest measure back of this heart searching, discomfort and warning; and first of all was the physical force which the Negro again and again and practically without ceasing from the first days of the slave trade down to the war of emancipation, used to effect his own freedom.

We must remember that the slave trade itself was war; that from surreptitious kidnapping of the unsuspecting it was finally organized so as to set African tribes warring against tribes, giving the conquerors the actual aid of European or Arabian soldiers and the tremendous incentive of high prices for results of successful wars through the selling of captives. The captives themselves fought to the last ditch. It is estimated

---

[42] Niles' Register, Vol. 16, May 22, 1819.
[43] Benjamin Brawley, *A Social History of the American Negro. New York, 1921, p. 90*

that every single slave finally landed upon a slave ship meant five corpses either left behind in Africa or lost through rebellion, suicide, sickness, and murder on the high seas. This which is so often looked upon as passive calamity was one of the most terrible and vindictive and unceasing struggles against misfortune that a group of human beings ever put forth. It cost Negro Africa perhaps sixty million souls to land ten million slaves in America.

The first influence of the Negro on American Democracy was naturally force to oppose force—revolt, murder, assassination coupled with running away. It was the primitive, ancient effort to avenge blood with blood, to bring good out of evil by opposing evil with evil. Whether right or wrong, effective or abortive, it is the human answer to oppression which the world has tried for thousands of years.

Two facts stand out in American history with regard to slave insurrections: on the one hand, there is no doubt of the continuous and abiding fear of them. The slave legislation of the Southern States is filled with ferocious efforts to guard against this. Masters were everywhere given peremptory and unquestioned power to kill a slave or even a white servant who should "resist his master." The Virginia law of 1680 said: "If any Negro or other slave shall absent himself from his master's service and lie, hide and lurk in obscure places, committing injuries to the inhabitants, and shall resist any person or persons that shall by lawful authority be employed to apprehend and take the said Negro, that then, in case of such resistance, it shall be lawful for such person or persons to kill the said Negro or slave so lying out and resisting."[44]

In 1691 and in 1748, there were Virginia acts to punish conspiracies and insurrections of slaves. In 1708 and in 1712 New York had laws against conspiracies and insurrections of Negroes. North Carolina passed such a law in 1741, and South Carolina in 1743 was legislating "against the insurrection and other wicked attempts of Negroes and other slaves." The Mississippi code of 1839 provides for slave insurrections "with arms in the intent to regain their liberty by

---

[44] Hening's Statutes.

force." Virginia in 1797 decreed death for any one exciting slaves to insurrection. In 1830 North Carolina made it a felony to incite insurrection among slaves. The penal code of Texas, passed in 1857, had a severe section against insurrection.[45]

Such legislation, common in every slave state, could not have been based on mere idle fear, and when we follow newspaper comment, debates and arguments and the history of insurrections and attempted insurrections among slaves, we easily see the reason. No sooner had the Negroes landed in America than resistance to slavery began.

As early as 1503 the Governor of Hispaniola stopped the transportation of Negroes "because they fled to the Indians and taught them bad manners and they could never be apprehended." In 1518 in the sugar mills of Haiti the Negroes "quit working and fled whenever they could in squads and started rebellions and committed murders." In 1522 there was a rebellion on the sugar plantations. Twenty Negroes from Diego Columbus' mill fled and killed several Spaniards. They joined with other rebellious Negroes on neighbouring plantations. In 1523 many Negro slaves "fled to the Zapoteca and walked rebelliously through the country." In 1527 there was an uprising of Indians and Negroes in Florida. In 1532 the Wolofs and other rebellious Negroes caused insurrection among the Carib Indians. These Wolofs were declared to be "haughty, disobedient, rebellious and incorrigible." In 1548 there was a rebellion in Honduras and the Viceroy Mendoza in Mexico writes of an uprising among the slaves and Indians in 1537.[46] One of the most remarkable cases of resistance was the establishment and defence of Palmares in Brazil where 40 determined Negroes in 1560 established a city state which lived for nearly a half century growing to a population of 20,000 and only overthrown when 7,000 soldiers with

---

[45] John C. Hurd, *The Law of Freedom and Bondage.* Boston, 1858-1862.
[46] Wiener, *Africa and the Discovery of America,* Bol. 1, pp. 155-8.

artillery were sent against it. The chiefs committed suicide rather than surrender.[47]

Early in the sixteenth century and from that time down until the nineteenth the black rebels whom the Spanish called "Cimarrones" and whom we know as "Maroons" were infesting the mountains and forests of the West Indies and South America. Gage says between 1520 and 1530: "What the Spaniards fear most until they get out of these mountains are two or three hundred Negroes, Cimarrones, who for the bad treatment they received have fled from masters in order to resort to these woods; there they live with their wives and children and increase in numbers every year, so that the entire force of Guatemala (City) and its environments is not capable to subdue them." Gage himself was captured by a mulatto corsair who was sweeping the seas in his own ship.[48]

The history of these Maroons reads like romance.[49] When England took Jamaica, in 1565, they found the mountains infested with Maroons whom they fought for ten years and finally, in 1663, acknowledged their freedom, gave them land and made their leader, Juan de Bolas, a colonel in the militia. He was killed, however, in the following year and from 1664 to 1778 some 3,000 black Maroons were in open rebellion against the British Empire. The English fought them with soldiers, Indians, and dogs and finally again, in 1738, made a formal treaty of peace with them, recognizing their freedom and granting them 25,000 acres of land. The war again broke out in 1795 and blood-hounds were again imported. The legislature wished to deport them but as they could not get their consent, peace was finally made on condition that the Maroons surrender their arms and settle down. No sooner, however, had they done this than the whites treacherously seized 600 of them and sent them to Nova Scotia. The Legislature voted a sword to the English

[47] C. E. Chapman, in *Journal of Negro History,* Vol. 1, pp. 392-8. More recent historical research indicates that the leaders of Palmares died fighting, but they did not generally commit suicide –Ed.

[48] J. Kunst, "Negroes in Guatemala," *Journal of Negro History,* Vol. 1, pp. 392-8.

[49] Cf. Bryan Edward's *West Indies,* 4th Edition, Vol. 1, pp. 337-98.

general, who made the treaty; but he indignantly refused to accept it. Eventually these Maroons were removed to Sierra Leone where they saved that colony to the British by helping them put down an insurrection.

In the United States insurrection and attempts at insurrection among the slaves extended from Colonial times down to the Civil War. For the most part they were unsuccessful. In many cases the conspiracies were insignificant in themselves but exaggerated by fear of the owners. And yet a record of the attempts at revolt large and small is striking.

In Virginia there was a conspiracy in 1710 in Surrey County. In 1712 the City of New York was threatened with burning by slaves. In 1720 whites were attacked in the homes and on the streets in Charleston, S. C. In 1730 both in South Carolina and Virginia, slaves were armed to kill the white people and they planned to burn the City of Boston in 1723. In 1730 there was an insurrection in Williamsburg, Va., and five counties furnished armed men. In 1730 and 1731 homes were burned by slaves in Massachusetts and in Rhode Island and in 1731 and 1732 three ships crews were murdered by slaves. In 1729 the Governor of Louisiana reported that in an expedition sent against the Indians, fifteen Negroes had "performed prodigies of valour." But the very next year the Indians, led by a desperate Negro named Samba, were trying to exterminate the whites.[50] In 1741 an insurrection of slaves was planned in New York City, for which thirteen slaves were burned, eighteen hanged and eighty transported. In 1754 and 1755 slaves burned and poisoned certain masters in Charleston, S. C.[51]

4. HAITI AND AFTER

On the night of August 23, 1791, the great Haitian rebellion took place. It had been preceded by a small rebellion of the mulattoes who were bitterly disappointed at the refusal of the planters to assent to what the free Negroes thought were the basic principles of the French Revolution.

---

[50] Gayarre, *History of Louisiana,* Vol. 1, pp. 435, 440.
[51] Du Bois's *Slave Trade,* pp. 6, 10, 22, 206 ; J. Coppin, *Slave Insurrections,* 1860; Brawley, *Social History,* pp.39, 86, 132.

When 450,000 slaves joined them, they began a murderous civil war seldom paralleled in history. French, English and Spaniards participated. Toussaint, the first great black leader, was deceived, imprisoned and died perhaps by poisoning. Twenty-five thousand French soldiers were sent over by Napoleon Bonaparte to subdue the Negroes and begin the extension of his American empire through the West Indies and up the Mississippi valley. Despite all this, the Negroes were triumphant, established an independent state, made Napoleon give up his dream of American empire and sell Louisiana for a song:[52] "Thus, all of Indian Territory, all of Kansas and Nebraska and Iowa and Wyoming and Montana and the Dakotas, and most of Colorado and Minnesota, and all of Washington and Oregon states, came to us as the indirect work of a despised Negro. Praise if you will, the work of Robert Livingston or a Jefferson, but today let us not forget our debt to Toussaint L'Ouverture, who was indirectly the means of America's expansion by the Louisiana Purchase of 1803."[53]

The Haitian revolution immediately had its effect upon both North and South America. We have read how Haitian volunteers helped in the American revolution. They returned to fight for their own freedom. Afterward when Bolivar, the founder of five free republics in South America, undertook his great rebellion in 1811 he at first failed. He took refuge in Jamaica and implored the help of England but was unsuccessful. Later in despair he visited Haiti. The black republic was itself at that time in a precarious position and had to act with great caution. Nevertheless President Pétion furnished Bolivar, soldiers, arms and money. Bolivar embarked secretly and again sought to free South America. Again he failed and a second time returned to Haiti. Money and reinforcements were a second time furnished him and with the help of these achieved the liberation of Mexico and Central America.

Thus black Haiti not only freed itself but helped to kindle liberty all through America. Refugees from Haiti and San Domingo poured into

---

[52] Cf. T. G. Steward, *The Haitian Revolution.*
[53] DeWitt Talmadge in the *Christian Herlad,* Nov. 28, 1906; Du Bois's *Slave Trade,* Chapter 7.

the United States both coloured and white and had great influence in Maryland and Louisiana.[54] Moreover the news of the black revolt filtered through to the slaves in the United States. Here the chains of slavery were stronger and the number of whites much larger. As I have said in another place: "A long, awful process of selection chose out the listless, ignorant, sly and humble and sent to heaven the proud, the vengeful and the daring. The old African warrior spirit died away of violence and a broken heart."[55]

Nevertheless a series of attempted rebellions took place which can be traced to the influence of Haiti. In 1800 came the Prosser conspiracy in Virginia which planned a force of 11,000 Negroes to march in three columns in the city and seize the arsenal. A terrific storm thwarted these men and thirty-six were executed for the attempt. In 1791 Negroes of Louisiana sought to imitate Toussaint leading to the execution of twenty-three slaves. Other smaller attempts were made in South Carolina in 1816 and in Georgia in 1819. In 1822 came the celebrated attempt of Denmark Vesey, an educated freedman who through his trade as carpenter accumulated considerable wealth. He spoke French and English and was familiar with the Haitian revolution, the African Colonization scheme and the agitation attending the Missouri compromise. He openly discussed slavery and ridiculed the slaves for their cowardice and submission; he worked through the church and planned the total annihilation of the men, women and children of Charleston. Thousands of slaves were enrolled but one betrayed him and this led to the arrest of 137 blacks of whom 35 were hanged and 37 banished. A white South Carolinian writing after this plot said: "We regard our Negroes as the Jacobins of the country, against whom we should always be upon our guard and who although we fear no permanent effects from any insurrectionary movements on their part, should be watched with an eye of steady and unremitted observation."[56]

---

[54] Cf. Dunbar-Nelson in the *Journal of Negro History,* Vol. 1.
[55] Du Bois, *John Brown,* p. 81.
[56] A. H. Grimke, *Right on the Scaffold,* in *Occasional Papers,* No. 7, American Negro Academy.

Less than ten years elapsed before another insurrection was planned and partially carried through. Its leader was Nat Turner, a slave born in Virginia in 1800. He was precocious and considered as "marked" by the Negroes. He had experimented in making paper, gun powder and pottery; never swore, never drank and never stole. For the most part he was a sort of religious devotee, fasting and praying and reading the Bible. Once he ran away but was commanded by spirit voices to return. By 1825 he was conscious of a great mission and on May 12, 1831, "a great voice said unto him that the serpent was loosed, that Christ had laid down the yoke." He believed that he, Nat Turner, was to lead the movement and that "the first should be last and the last first." An eclipse of the sun in February, 1831 was a further sign to him. He worked quickly. Gathering six friends together August 21, they made their plans and then started the insurrection by killing Nat's master and the family. About forty Negroes were gathered in all and they killed sixty-one white men, women and children. They were headed toward town when finally the whites began to arm in opposition. It was not, however, until two months later, October 30, that Turner himself was captured. He was tried November 5 and sentenced to be hanged. When asked if he believed in the righteousness of his mission he replied "Was not Christ crucified?" He made no confession.[57]

T. R. Grey—Turner's attorney—said "As to his ignorance, he certainly had not the advantages of education, but he can read and write and for natural intelligence and quickness of apprehension is surpassed by few men I have ever seen. Further the calm, deliberate composure with which he spoke of his late deeds and intentions, the expression of his fiend-like face when excited by enthusiasm; still bearing the stains of the blood of helpless innocence about him; clothed with rags and covered with chains, yet daring to raise his manacled hands to heaven; with a spirit soaring above the attributes of man, I looked on him and my blood curdled in my veins."[58]

---

[57] Brawley, p. 140; T. W. Higginson, Atlantic Monthly, *Vol. 8, p. 173.*
[58] I. W. Cromwell, in *Journal of Negro History,* Vol. 5, pp. 208 ff.

Panic seized the whole of Virginia and the South. Military companies were mobilized, both whites and Negroes fled to the swamps, slaves were imprisoned and even as far down as Macon, Georgia, the white women and children were guarded in a building against supposed insurrections. New slave codes were adopted, new disabilities put upon freedmen, the carrying of fire arms was especially forbidden. The Negro churches in the South were almost stopped from functioning and the Negro preachers from preaching. Traveling and meeting of slaves was stopped, learning to read and write was forbidden and incendiary pamphlets hunted down. Free Negroes were especially hounded, sold into slavery or driven out and a period of the worst oppression of the Negro in the land followed.

In 1839 and 1841 two cases of mutiny of slaves on the high seas caused much commotion in America. In 1839 a schooner, the *Amistad*, started from Havana for another West Indian port with 53 slaves. Led by a black man, Cinque, the slaves rose, killed the captain and some of the crew, allowed the rest of the crew to escape and put the two owners in irons. The Negroes then tried to escape to Africa, but after about two months they landed in Connecticut and a celebrated law case arose over the disposition of the black mutineers which went to the Supreme Court of the United States. John Quincy Adams defended them and won his case. Eventually money was raised and the Negroes returned to Africa. While this case was in the court the brig Creole in 1841 sailed from Richmond to New Orleans with 130 slaves. Nineteen of the slaves mutinied and led by Madison Washington took command of the vessel and sailed to the British West Indies. Daniel Webster demanded the return of the slaves but the British authorities refused.

During these years, rebellion and agitation among Negroes, and agitation among white friends in Europe, was rapidly freeing the Negroes of the West Indies and beginning their incorporation into the body politic— a process not yet finished but which means possibly the eventual development of a free black and mulatto republic in the isles of the Caribbean.

Fig. 5. *La Amistad*

It may be said that in most of these cases the attempts of the Negro to rebel were abortive, and this is true. Yet it must be remembered that in a few cases they had horrible success; in others nothing but accident or the actions of favourite slaves saved similar catastrophe, and more and more the white South had the feeling that it was sitting upon a volcano and that nothing but the sternest sort of repression would keep the Negro "in his place." The appeal of the Negro to force invited reaction and retaliation not only in the South, as we have noted, but also in the North. Here the common white workingman and particularly the new English, Scotch and Irish immigrants entirely misconceived the writhing of the black man. These white labourers, themselves so near slavery, did not recognize the struggle of the black slave as part of their own struggle; rather they felt the sting of economic rivalry and underbidding for home and job; they easily absorbed hatred and contempt for Negroes as their first American lesson and were flattered by the white capitalists, slave owners and sympathizers with slavery into lynching and clubbing their dark fellow victims back into the pit whence they sought to crawl. It was a scene for angels' tears.

In 1826 Negroes were attacked in Cincinnati and also in 1836 and 1841. At Portsmouth, Ohio, nearly one-half of the Negroes were driven out of the city in 1830 while mobs drove away free Negroes from Mercer County, Ohio. In Philadelphia, Negroes were attacked in 1820, 1830 and 1834, having their churches and property burned and ruined. In 1838 there was another anti-Negro riot and in 1842, when the blacks attempted to celebrate abolition in the West Indies. Pittsburgh had a riot in 1839 and New York in 1843 and 1863.[59]

Thus we can see that the fear and heart searchings and mental upheaval of those who saw the anomaly of slavery in the United States was based not only upon theoretical democracy but on force and fear of force as used by the degraded blacks, and on the reaction of that appeal on southern legislatures and northern mobs.

5. THE APPEAL TO REASON

The appeal of the Negro to democracy, however, was not entirely or perhaps even principally an appeal of force. There was continually the appeal to reason and justice. Take the significant case of Paul Cuffee of Massachusetts, born in 1759, of a Negro father and Indian mother. When the selectmen of the town of Dartmouth refused to admit coloured children to the public schools, or even to make separate provision for them, he refused to pay his school taxes. He was duly imprisoned, but when freed he built at his own expense a school house and opened it to all without race discrimination. His white neighbours were glad to avail themselves of this school as it was more convenient and just as good as the school in town. The result was that the coloured children were soon admitted to all schools. Cuffee was a ship owner and trader, and afterward took a colony to Liberia at his own expense.[60] Again Prince Hall, the Negro founder of the African Lodge of Masons which the English set up in 1775, aroused by the revolution in Haiti and a race riot in Boston said in 1797:

---

[59] Cf. Du Bois's *Philadelphia Negro*, Chapter 4; Woodson's *Negro in our History*, pp. 140-1.
[60] Brawley, pp. 123-4; *Journal of Negro History*, Vol. 2, pp. 209-28.

"Patience, I say, for were we not possessed of a great measure of it you could not bear up under the daily insults you meet with in the streets of Boston; much more on public days of recreation, how are you shamefully abused, and that at such a degree that you may truly be said to carry your lives in your own hands....

"My brethren, let us not be cast down under these and many other abuses we at present labour under; for the darkest hour is before the break of day. My brethren, let us remember what a dark day it was with our African brethren six years ago, in the French West Indies.... But blessed be to God, the scene is changed, they now confess that God hath no respect of persons, and therefore receive them as their friends and treat them as brothers. Thus doth Ethiopia begin to stretch forth her hand from a sink of slavery to freedom and equality."[61]

A more subtle appeal was made by seven Massachusetts Negroes on taxation without representation. In a petition to the General Court of Massachusetts in 1780 they said: "We being chiefly of the African extract, and by reason of long bondage and hard slavery, we have been deprived of enjoying the profits of our labour or the advantage of inheriting estates from our parents, as our neighbours the white people do, having some of us not long enjoyed our own freedom; yet of late, contrary to the invariable custom and practice of the country, we have been, and now are, taxed both in our polls and that small pittance of estate which, through much hard labour and industry, we have got together to sustain ourselves and families withal. We apprehend it therefore, to be hard usage, and will doubtless (if continued) reduce us to a state of beggary, whereby we shall become a burden to others, if not timely prevented by the interposition of your justice and power.

"Your petitioners further show, that we apprehend ourselves to be aggrieved, in that, while we are not allowed the privilege of free men of the State, having no vote or influence in the election of those that tax us, yet many of our colour (as is well known) have cheerfully entered the field of battle in the defence of the common cause, and that (as we

---

[61] Brawley, p. 71.

conceive) against similar exertion of power (in regard to taxation) too well known to need a recital in this place."[62]

Perhaps though the most startling appeal and challenge came from David Walker, a free Negro, born of a free mother and slave father in North Carolina in 1785. He had some education, had travelled widely and conducted a second-hand clothing store in Boston in 1827. He spoke to various audiences of Negroes in 1828 and the following year published the celebrated "Appeal in four articles, together with a preamble to the Coloured Citizens of the World but in particular and very expressly to those of the United States of America." It was a thin volume of 76 octavo pages, but it was frank and startlingly clear:

"Can our condition be any worse? Can it be more mean and abject? If there are any changes, will they not be for the better though they may appear for the worst at first? Can they get us any lower? Where can they get us? They cannot treat us worse; for they well know the day they do it they are gone. But against all accusations which may or can be preferred against me, I appeal to heaven for my motive in writing—who knows that my object is if possible to awaken in the breasts of my afflicted, degraded and slumbering brethren a spirit of enquiry and investigation respecting our miseries and wretchedness in this Republican land of Liberty!!!!

"My beloved brethren:—The Indians of North and South America—the Greeks—the Irish, subjected under the King of Great Britain—the Jews, that ancient people of the Lord—the inhabitants of the Islands of the Sea—in fine, all the inhabitants of the Earth, (except, however, the sons of Africa) are called men and of course are and ought to be free.—But we, (coloured people) and our children are brutes and of course are and ought to be slaves to the American people and their children forever—to dig their mines and work their farms; and thus go on enriching them from one generation to another with our blood and our tears!!!!

---

[62] Williams' *Negro Race,* Vol. 2, p. 126.

"I saw a paragraph, a few years since, in a South Carolina paper, which, speaking of the barbarity of the Turks, it said: 'The Turks are the most barbarous people in the world—they treat the Greeks more like brutes than human beings.' And in the same paper was an advertisement which said: 'Eight well built Virginia and Maryland Negro fellows and four wenches will positively be sold this day to the highest bidder!'

"Beloved brethren—here let me tell you, and believe it, that the Lord our God as true as He sits on His throne in heaven and as true as our Saviour died to redeem the world, will give you a Hannibal, and when the Lord shall have raised him up and given him to you for your possession, Oh! my suffering brethren, remember the divisions and consequent sufferings of Carthage and of Haiti. Read the history particularly of Haiti and see how they were butchered by the whites and do you take warning. The person whom God shall give you, give him your support and let him go his length and behold in him the salvation of your God. God will indeed deliver you through him from your deplorable and wretched condition under the Christians of America. I charge you this day before my God to lay no obstacle in his way, but let him go.... What the American preachers can think of us, I aver this day before my God I have never been able to define. They have newspapers and monthly periodicals which they receive in continual succession but on the pages of which you will scarcely ever find a paragraph respecting slavery which is ten thousand times more injurious to this country than all the other evils put together; and which will be the final overthrow of its government unless something is very speedily done; for their cup is nearly full.—Perhaps they will laugh at or make light of this; but I tell you, Americans! that unless you speedily alter your course, you and your Country are gone!

"Do you understand your own language? Hear your language proclaimed to the world, July 4, 1776—'We hold these truths to be self evident—that ALL men are created EQUAL!! That they are endowed by their Creator with certain unalienable rights; that among these are life, liberty and the pursuit of happiness!!! Compare your own language above, extracted from your Declaration of Independence, with your cruelties and murders inflicted by your cruel and unmerciful fathers and yourselves on our fathers and on us—men who have never given your fathers or you the least provocation!!!

"Now Americans! I ask you candidly, was your suffering under Great Britain one hundredth part as cruel and tyrannical as you have rendered ours under you? Some of you, no doubt, believe that we will never throw off your murderous government and provide new guards for our future 'security'. If Satan has made you believe it, will he not deceive you?"

The book had a remarkable career. It appeared in September, was in a third edition by the following March and aroused the South to fury. Special laws were passed and demands made that Walker be punished. He died in 1830, possibly by foul play.

6. THE FUGITIVE SLAVE

Beside force and the appeal to reason there was a third method which practically was more effective and decisive for eventual abolition, and that was the escape from slavery through running away. On the islands this meant escape to the mountains and existence as brigands. In South America it meant escape to the almost impenetrable forest.

As I have said elsewhere:[63]

"One thing saved the South from the blood sacrifice of Haiti—not, to be sure, from so successful a revolt, for the disproportion of races was less, but from a desperate and bloody effort—and that was the escape of the fugitive.

"Along the Great Black Way stretched swamps and rivers and the forests and crests of the Alleghanies. A widening, hurrying stream of fugitives swept to the havens of refuge, taking the restless, the criminal and the unconquered—the natural leaders of the more timid mass. These men saved slavery and killed it. They saved it by leaving it to a false seductive dream of peace and the eternal subjugation of the labouring

---

[63] Du Bois's *John Brown*, pp. 82 ff.

class. They destroyed it by presenting themselves before the eyes of the North and the world as living specimens of the real meaning of slavery."

"Three paths were opened to the slaves: to submit, to fight or to run away. Most of them submitted, as do most people everywhere, to force and fate. To fight singly meant death and to fight together meant plot and insurrection—a difficult thing, but one often tried. Easiest of all was to run away, for the land was wide and bare and the slaves were many. At first they ran to the swamps and mountains and starved and died. Then they ran to the Indians and in Florida founded a nation, to overthrow which cost the United States $20,000,000 and more in slave raids known as the Seminole 'wars.' Then gradually, after the War of 1812 had used so many black sailors to fight for free trade that the Negroes learned of the North and Canada as cities of refuge, they fled northward."

From the sixteenth century Florida Indians had Negro blood, but from early part of the nineteenth century the Seminoles gained a large new infiltration of Negro blood from the numbers of slaves who fled to them and with whom they intermarried. The first Seminole war, therefore, in 1818 was not simply a defence of the frontiers against the Indians and a successful raid to drive Spain from Florida, it was also a slave raid by Georgia owners determined to have back their property. By 1815 Negroes from Georgia among the Creeks and Seminoles numbered not less than 11,000 and were settled along the Appalachicola river, many of them with good farms and with a so-called Negro "fort" for protection. The war was disastrous to Negroes and Indians but not fatal and in 1822 some 800 Negroes were counted among the Indians who inhabited the new territory seized from Spain. Pressure to secure alleged fugitives and Negroes from the Indians was kept up for the next three years and the second Seminole war broke out because the whites treacherously seized the mulatto wife of the Indian chief Osceola. The war broke out in 1837 and its real nature, as a New Orleans paper said in 1839, was to subdue the Seminoles and decrease the danger of uprisings "among the serviles." Finally after a total cost of twenty million dollars the Indians were subdued and moved to the West and a part of the Negroes driven back into slavery, but not all.[64]

Through the organization which came to be known as the Underground Railroad, thousands of slaves escaped through Kentucky and into the Middle West and thence into Canada and also by way of the Appalachian Mountains into Pennsylvania and the East. Not only were they helped by white abolitionists but they were guided by black men and women like Joshua Henson and Harriet Tubman.

Beside this there came the effort for emigration to Africa which was very early suggested. Two coloured men sailed from New York for Africa in 1774 but the Revolutionary War stopped the effort thus begun. The Virginia legislature in secret session after Gabriel's insurrection in 1800, tried to suggest the buying of some land for the colonization of free Negroes, following the proposal of Thomas Jefferson made in 1781. Paul Cuffee, mentioned above, started the actual migration in 1815 carrying nine coloured families, thirty-eight persons in all, to Sierra Leone at an expense of $4,000 which he paid himself. Finally came the American Colonization Society in 1817 but it was immediately turned from a real effort to abolish slavery gradually into an effort to get rid of free Negroes and obstreperous slaves. Even the South saw it and Robert Y. Hayne said in Congress: "While this process is going on, the coloured classes are gradually diffusing themselves throughout the country and are making steady advances in intelligence and refinement and if half the zeal were displayed in bettering their condition that is now wasted in the vain and fruitless effort of sending them abroad, their intellectual and moral improvement would be steady and rapid."

---

[64] Cf. Joshua R. Giddings, *Exiles of Florida,* Columbus, Ohio, 1858.

7. BARGAINING

The Negro early learned a lesson which he may yet teach the modern world and which may prove his crowning gift to America and the world: Force begets force and you cannot in the end run away successfully from the world's problems. The Negro early developed the shrewd foresight of recognizing the fact that as a minority of black folk in a growing white country, he could not win his battle by force. Moreover, for the mass of Negroes, it was impracticable to run away and find refuge in some other land.

Even the appeal to reason had its limitations in an unreasoning land. It could not unfortunately base itself on justice and right in the midst of the selfish, breathless battle to earn a living. There was however a chance to prove that justice and self interest sometimes go hand in hand. Force and flight might sometimes help but there was still the important method of co-operating with the best forces of the nation in order to help them to win and in order to prove that the Negro was a valuable asset, not simply as a labourer but as a worker for social uplift, as an American. Sometimes this co-operation was in simple and humble ways and nevertheless striking. There was, for instance, the yellow fever epidemic in Philadelphia in 1793. The blacks were not suffering from it or at least not supposed to suffer from it as much as the whites. The papers appealed to them to come forward and help with the sick. Led by Jones, Gray and Allen, Negroes volunteered their services and worked with the sick and in burying the dead, even spending some of their own funds in the gruesome duty. The same thing happened much later in New Orleans, Memphis and Cuba.

In larger ways it must be remembered that the Abolition crusade itself could not have been successful without the co-operation of Negroes. Black folk like Remond, Frederick Douglass, and Sojourner Truth, were not simply advocates for freedom but were themselves living refutations of the whole doctrine of slavery. Their appeal was tremendous in its efficiency and besides, the free Negroes helped by work and money to spread the Abolition campaign.[65]

In addition to this there was much deliberate bargaining,— careful calculation on the part of the Negro that if the whites would aid them, they in turn would aid the whites at critical times and that otherwise they would not. Much of this went on at the time of the Revolution and was clearly recognized by the whites.

Alexander Hamilton (himself probably of Negro descent) said in 1779: "The contempt we have been taught to entertain for the blacks makes us fancy many things that are founded neither in reason nor experience; and an unwillingness to part with property of so valuable a kind will furnish a thousand arguments to show the impracticability or pernicious tendency of a scheme which requires such a sacrifice. But it should be considered that if we do not make use of them in this way, the enemy probably will; and that the best way to counteract the temptations they will hold out will be to offer them ourselves. An essential part of the plan is to give them their freedom with their muskets. This will secure their fidelity, animate their courage, and, I believe, will have a good influence upon those who remain by opening a door to their emancipation. This circumstance, I confess, has no small weight in inducing me to wish the success of the project; for the dictates of humanity and true policy equally interest me in favour of this unfortunate class of men."[66]

Dr Hopkins wrote in 1776: "God is so ordering it in His providence that it seems absolutely necessary something should speedily be done with respect to the slaves among us in order to our safety and to prevent their turning against us in our present struggle in order to get their liberty. Our oppressors have planned to gain the blacks and induce them to take up arms against us by promising them liberty on this condition; and this plan they are prosecuting to the utmost of their power.... The only way pointed out to prevent this threatening evil is to

---

[65] Among the first subscribers to Garrison's *Liberator* were free Negroes and one report is that the very first paid subscriber was a coloured Philadelphia caterer.
[66] Livermore, p. 170.

set the blacks at liberty ourselves by some public acts and laws; and then give them proper encouragement to labour or take arms in the defence of the American cause, as they shall choose. This would at once be doing them some degree of justice and defeating our enemies in the scheme they are prosecuting."[67]

When Dunmore appealed to the slaves of Virginia at the beginning of the Revolution, the slave owners issued an almost plaintive counter appeal:

"Can it, then, be supposed that the Negroes will be better used by the English who have always encouraged and upheld this slavery than by their present masters who pity their condition; who wish, in general, to make it easy and comfortable as possible; and who would, were it in their power, or were they permitted, not only prevent any more Negroes from losing their freedom but restore it to such as have already unhappily lost it?"[68]

In the South, where Negroes for the most part were not received as soldiers, the losses of the slaveholders by defection among the slaves was tremendous. John Adams says that the Georgia delegates gave him "a melancholy account of the State of Georgia and South Carolina. They said if one thousand regular troops should land in Georgia and their commander be provided with arms and clothes enough and proclaim freedom to all the Negroes who would join his camp, twenty thousand Negroes would join it from the two provinces in a fortnight. The Negroes have a wonderful art of communicating intelligence among themselves; it will run several hundreds of miles in a week or fortnight. They said their only security was this,—that all the King's friends and tools of Government have large plantations and property in Negroes, so that the slaves of the Tories would be lost as well as those of the Whigs."[69]

---

[67] Livermore, pp. 125-6.
[68] Force's Archives, 4th series, Vol. 3, p. 1387.
[69] Works of John Adams, Vol. 2, p. 428.

Great Britain, after Cornwallis surrendered, even dreamed of reconquering America with Negroes. A Tory wrote to Lord Dunmore in 1782:

"If, my Lord, this scheme is adopted, arranged and ready for being put in execution, the moment the troops penetrate into the country after the arrival of the promised re-enforcements, America is to be conquered with its own force (I mean the Provincial troops and the black troops to be raised), and the British and Hessian army could be spared to attack the French where they are most vulnerable...."

"'What! Arm the slaves? We shudder at the very idea, so repugnant to humanity, so barbarous and shocking to human nature,' etc. One very simple answer is, in my mind, to be given: Whether it is better to make this vast continent become an acquisition of power, strength and consequence to Great Britain again, or tamely give it up to France who will reap the fruits of American independence to the utter ruin of Britain? ... experience will, I doubt not, justify the assertion that by embodying the most hardy, intrepid and determined blacks, they would not only keep the rest in good order but by being disciplined and under command be prevented from raising cabals, tumults, and even rebellion, what I think might be expected soon after a peace; but so far from making even our lukewarm friends and secret foes greater enemies by this measure, I will, by taking their slaves, engage to make them better friends."[70]

On the other hand, the Colonial General Greene wrote to the Governor of South Carolina the same year:

"The natural strength of the country in point of numbers appears to me to consist much more in the blacks than in the whites. Could they be incorporated and employed for its defence, it would afford you double security. That they would make good soldiers, I have not the least doubt; and I am persuaded the State has it not in its power to give sufficient re-enforcements without incorporating them either to secure the country if the enemy mean to act vigorously upon an offensive plan

---

[70] Livermore, pp. 183, 184.

or furnish a force sufficient to dispossess them of Charleston should it be defensive."

This spirit of bargaining, more or less carefully carried out, can be seen in every time of stress and war. During the Civil War certain groups of Negroes sought repeatedly to make terms with the Confederacy. Judah Benjamin said at a public meeting in Richmond in 1865:

"We have 680,000 blacks capable of bearing arms and who ought now to be in the field. Let us now say to every Negro who wishes to go into the ranks on condition of being free, go and fight—you are free. My own Negroes have been to me and said, 'Master, set us free and we'll fight for you.' You must make up your minds to try this or see your army withdrawn from before your town. I know not where white men can be found."[71]

Robert E. Lee said: "We should not expect slaves to fight for prospective freedom when they can secure it at once by going to the enemy in whose service they will incur no greater risk than in ours. The reasons that induce me to recommend the employment of Negro troops at all render the effect of the measures I have suggested upon slavery immaterial and in my opinion the best means of securing the efficiency and fidelity of the auxiliary force would be to accompany the measure with a well-digested plan of gradual and general emancipation. As that will be the result of the continuance of the war and will certainly occur if the enemy succeed, it seems to me most advisable to adopt it at once and thereby obtain all the benefits that will accrue to our cause.

"The employment of Negro troops under regulations similar to those indicated would, in my opinion, greatly increase our military strength and enable us to relieve our white population to some extent. I think we could dispense with the reserve forces except in cases of emergency. It would disappoint the hopes which our enemies have upon our exhaustion, deprive them in a great measure of the aid they now derive from black troops and thus throw the burden of the war upon

---

[71] Wilson, pp. 491-92.

their own people. In addition to the great political advantages that would result to our cause from the adoption of a system of emancipation, it would exercise a salutary influence upon our Negro population by rendering more secure the fidelity of those who become soldiers and diminishing inducements to the rest to abscond."[72]

At the time of the World War there was a distinct attitude on the part of the Negro population that unless they were recognized in the draft and had Negro officers and were not forced to become simply labourers, they would not fight and while expression of this determination was not always made openly it was recognized even by an administration dominated by Southerners. Especially were there widespread rumours of German intrigue among Negroes, which had some basis of fact.

Within the Negro group every effort for organization and uplift was naturally an effort toward the development of American democracy. The motive force of democracy has nearly always been the push from below rather than the aristocratic pull from above; the effort of the privileged classes to outstrip the surging forward of the bourgeoisie has made groups and nations rise; the determination of the "poor whites" in the South not to be outdone by the "nigger" has been caused by the black man's frantic efforts to rise rather than by any innate ambition on the part of the lower class of whites. It was a push from below and it made the necessity of recognizing the white labourer even more apparent. The great democratic movement which took place during the reign of Andrew Jackson from 1829-1837 was caused in no small degree by the persistent striving of the Negroes. They began their meeting together in conventions in 1830, they organized migration to Canada.[73] In the trouble with Canada in 1837 and 1838 Negro refugees from America helped to defend the frontiers. Bishop Loguen says: "The coloured population of Canada at that time was small compared to what it now is; nevertheless, it was sufficiently large to attract the attention of

---

[72] J. T. Wilson, *The History of the Black Phalanx,* Hartford, 1897, p. 490.
[73] Cf. Cromwell, *Negro in American History,* Chapter 2.

the government. They were almost to a man fugitives from the States. They could not, therefore, be passive when the success of the invaders would break the only arm interposed for their security, and destroy the only asylum for African freedom in North America. The promptness with which several companies of blacks were organized and equipped, and the desperate valour they displayed in this brief conflict, are an earnest of what may be expected from the welling thousands of coloured fugitives collecting there, in the event of a war between the two countries."[74]

In America during this time they sought to establish a manual training college, they established their first weekly newspaper and they made a desperate fight for admission to the schools. They helped thus immeasurably the movement for universal popular education, joined the anti-slavery societies and organized churches and beneficial societies; bought land and continued to appeal. Wealthy free Negroes began to appear even in the South, as in the case of Jehu Jones, proprietor of a popular hotel in Charleston, and later Thomé Lafon of New Orleans who accumulated nearly a half million dollars and eventually left it to Negro charities which still exist. In the North there were tailors and lumber merchants and the guild of the caterers; taxable property slowly but surely increased.

All this in a peculiar way forced a more all-embracing democracy upon America, and it blossomed to fuller efficiency after the Civil War.

---

[74] J. W. Loguen, *As a Slave and as a Freeman*, p. 344.

8. Elizabeth Ross Haynes

HARRIET TUBMAN
The Moses of Her People
1820-1913[1]

About one hundred years ago, people in every civilized country were talking about the "underground railroad" in the United States. The "underground railroad" was not really a railroad under the ground, but a secret way by means of which slaves escaped from their masters in the South and reached free territory. Reaching free territory sometimes

---

[1] Extract from Chapter IV of *Unsung Heroes.*

meant escape from this country into Canada. Passengers, those seeking
to escape to free territory, on the "underground railroad" were led by
very brave and daring conductors. Among these conductors there was a
woman whose name was Harriet Tubman.

When Harriet was born in Dorchester County, Maryland, in
1820, she was named Araminta Ross. After she grew up, she called
herself Harriet. When she became a woman she was married to John
Tubman and was called Harriet Tubman.

Harriet almost died with the measles when she was six years old.
Soon after she recovered from this, her master threw a heavy weight at
her and injured her skull. For years she suffered from pressure on her
brain which caused her to fall asleep at any time, wherever she was,
whether she was seated on a rail fence or in a chair. It also caused her to
stagger sometimes as she walked. No one except her African mother
seemed to care for her or to pay any attention to her.

Early one morning a lady came driving up to the home of
Harriet's master, who met her at the gate and inquired what he could do
for her. She asked for a slave-girl to care for her baby, but offered very
low wages. The master shook his head, saying, "I cannot furnish you a
girl for that." As the lady pleaded with him, he stood looking on the
ground and knitting his brow. Suddenly he lifted his head and said, "Yes,
I have just one girl whom you may take; keep your eye on her because
she may not have all that is coming to her." Harriet was called, placed in
a wagon and driven away to the lady's home.

The first thing the lady gave her to do was to sweep and dust the
parlour. Harriet cautiously tiptoed into this wonderfully fine room,
amazed at everything she saw. She finally began to sweep in much the
same way as she had swept her mother's cabin. As soon as she had
finished sweeping, she took the dusting cloth and wiped off the chairs,
the table, and the mantelpiece. The particles of dust, still flying here and
there over the room, soon settled on the furniture again.

About this time, Harriet's new mistress stepped in and began to
look around. The dust lay on the table, the chairs, and the mantel in such
a thick coating that she spoke very harshly to Harriet and ordered her to

do the work all over. Harriet swept and dusted just as she had done before. The dust, having no other place to go, settled again on the furniture. The mistress entered the parlour again, bringing with her this time a whip. With this, she lashed Harriet with a heavy hand. Five times before breakfast that morning Harriet swept and dusted the parlour.

Just as she had got her third whipping, her mistress's sister, who had been awakened from her morning slumber, opened the parlour door. "Why do you whip the child, sister, for not doing what she has never been taught to do?" she asked. "Leave Harriet to me for a few minutes and you will see that she will soon learn how to sweep and dust a room."

The sister ordered Harriet to open the windows first, to sweep the room and leave it awhile until the dust settled, and to return then and wipe the dust from the furniture.

Harriet looked strangely at the big window, went to it and raised it inch by inch until it was high enough to fasten by a latch. She set it in again and swept, and while the dust was settling, she went out and set the table for breakfast. Then she returned and dusted the parlour.

That night she was ordered to sit up and rock the baby. The baby's cradle and Harriet's chair were placed near her mistress's bed. Occasionally Harriet's eyelids dropped and her head bobbed this way and that way. The cradle kept on rocking because her foot was on the rockers. Once in a great while, the cradle would stop and the baby would begin to cry. The mistress would pick up her whip and give Harriet a cut across the head and shoulders which would make her jump and almost knock the cradle over.

Under such treatment, Harriet became so worn and thin that the lady sent her back to her master saying that she wasn't worth a six-pence. Harriet was turned over to her mother, who nursed her until she was again strong enough to work.

She was then hired out to a man who made her plough, drive oxen, lift a barrel of flour, and sometimes cut a half cord of wood a day. Soon she became ill again. She lay on her sick-bed from Christmas until March. Day after day she prayed, saying, "O Lord, convert old Master;

change that man's heart and make him a Christian." When someone told her that as soon as she was able to work, she would be sent away, she changed her prayer, saying: "Lord, if you are never going to change that man's heart, kill him, Lord, and take him out of the way, so he will do no more mischief." Harriet's master finally died but she continued ill for a long time.

Even after she became stronger she still prayed at every turn. When she went to the horse-trough to wash her face and hands, she said, "Lord, wash me and make me clean." When she took the towel to wipe them, she cried, "O Lord, for Jesus' sake, wipe away all my sins." When she took up the broom to sweep, she groaned, "O Lord, whatever sin there is in my heart, sweep it out, Lord, clear and clean."

Early one morning many of the slaves in the "quarters" hurried about with a scared look on their faces, whispering something to each other as they passed. The news had leaked out that Harriet and two of her brothers were to be sold and sent the next day to the far South. As soon as the news reached Harriet, she held a hurried consultation with her brothers, telling them of the terrible things that would befall them if they did not run away to the North. As they stood for a while looking about anxiously and ready to move on, they agreed to start for the North that night.

Harriet began to scratch her head and wonder how she might tell her friends that she was going away. She thought and thought, and finally hit upon the plan of telling then in an old familiar song. As she was passing the next cabin door she sang out:

When that old chariot comes,
I'm going to leave you;
I'm bound for the promised land.
Friends, I'm going to leave you.
I'm sorry, friends, to leave you,
Farewell! Oh, farewell!
But I'll meet you in the morning!
Farewell! Oh, farewell!

THE NEED FOR HEROES

She looked forward and backward and all around several times. No overseer was in sight. She continued to sing, casting a meaning glance at first one and then another as she passed along:

I'll meet you in the morning,
When you reach the promised land,
On the other side of Jordan,
For I'm bound for the promised land.

That night, Harriet and her brothers spoke for a while in a whisper to their father and kissed him goodbye. Without disturbing their dear old mother, each started out quietly in slightly different directions, but all towards the same place. Soon the three came together. The brothers began to say to Harriet in very low tones that they were afraid that old master would send men out for them and capture them. They stood trembling with excitement. All at once, one of them and then the other broke away and ran towards home as fast as they could, falling now and then over a log or a stump. Harriet stood watching them as long as she could see their shadows in the starlight.

Fixing her eye on the North Star, she turned her face in that direction and went forward. All night long she walked until the peep of day, then she lay down in the tall grass in a swamp. She lay there all day. The next night she started out again. Night after night she travelled, occasionally stopping to beg bread. She crouched behind trees or lay concealed in a swamp during the day until she reached Philadelphia.

On her arrival in Philadelphia she stared at the people as they passed. She stood gazing at the fine houses and the streets. She looked at her hands, believing that they, too, looked new. After finding a place to stay, she walked out among the better looking houses and began to ask from door to door if anyone was needed for work. Finally a woman came to the door, opened it just a little way and peeped out as though she were afraid. As Harriet was asking for work, the lady told her to wait a moment while she ran back and pushed her frying pan further back on the stove. She appeared again at the door, questioned Harriet and then told her to come in.

Harriet walked in and stood listening to the lady's instructions about cleaning. Then she raised the windows and began to sweep. She swept and dusted and cleaned all day. She worked hard the next day and every day until pay-day, when she received her first money. She hid it away with great care and continued her work. The following pay-days she went to the same spot and hid away every penny of her money until she felt that she had enough to go back South.

She gave up her work and travelled night after night until she was again back on the plantation. She hid around among the slaves in their cabins. She whispered to them thrilling stories of the free country, until even women with babies were getting ready to follow her back to the North. After drugging their babies with paregoric and placing them in baskets which they carried on their arms, they set out with "Moses," as they called her, for the free country.

They forded rivers, climbed mountains, went through swamps, threaded the forests with their feet sore and often bleeding. They travelled during the night and kept in hiding during the day. One of the men fell by the wayside. Harriet took out her pistol, and pointing it at his head, said, "Dead men tell no tales; you go on or die!" He arose trembling and dragged along with the party until they reached the North.

As soon as Harriet had landed this party, she began working again and making preparations to go back on her next trip. One night she went back to the plantation, secured a horse and a two-wheel cart and drove away with her aged mother and father. After placing them on the train, she travelled in the cart night after night until she made her way through Maryland to Wilmington, Delaware, where she had sent her parents.

As soon as the three of them met in Wilmington, Harriet took her parents to a well-known underground railroad station. This was simply the home of a Quaker friend. He gave them food and shelter and each a new pair of shoes. He furnished Harriet with money to take her parents on to Canada, and kept the horse and cart for sale. Harriet and her parents went on, making their way with difficulty, until they reached Canada.

Harriet remained in Canada for a short time only, then slipped back among the plantation cabins in Maryland. Again and again she went back—nineteen times—leading away in the darkness, in all, over three hundred slaves. The slave masters in that region in Maryland, whence so many were being stolen away, after trying hard to catch Harriet, offered a reward of $40,000 for her, dead or alive. They posted such a notice in all public places....

[At the outbreak of the U.S. Civil War], Governor Andrew of Massachusetts sent for her. He asked if she would go South as a spy and a scout, and if need be, a hospital nurse for the Union soldiers. She stood thinking for a moment, then said that she would go. He bade her return home and be ready at a moment's notice....

Soon after she reached home, a messenger arrived with orders for her to report immediately. She hastily grabbed a few necessary things, kissed her parents, saying good-bye...and hurried away to join a company of soldiers on its way South. They travelled several days. As soon as they arrived, Harriet was ordered to act as a scout and a spy for the soldiers. She took charge and led them through the jungle and the swamp. She approached the frightened slaves, often gaining valuable information from them. She stood in the battle-line when the shots were falling like hail and the bodies of dead and wounded men were dropping like leaves in autumn....

TOUSSAINT L'OUVERTURE
Commander-in-Chief of an Army
President of Hayti
1743-1803[2]

Trouble arose among [enslaved Africans, free Blacks, Frenchmen, and Spaniards] and war broke out. For days fires raged, houses were burned and thousands of people fell dead and mortally wounded by bullets. Toussaint looked on, but took no part in the war at first. When his master's home was about to be burned to the ground he broke into it, rescued very valuable articles for his master, and helped his master's family to escape from the island. Then he became a free man, joined the army of slaves, and soon rose to the rank of colonel. His army joined with the Spaniards, but when the French gave freedom to all the slaves, his army joined the French and drove the Spaniards from the island

Before the close of the war, the French made Toussaint brigadier-general. As brigadier-general he made charts of the island and studied them so closely that he knew the course of every stream and the location of every hill.

He fought the Spanish so hard that one after another their towns fell into the hands of the French. One day a French soldier exclaimed, *"Cet homme fait overture partout"* (this man makes an opening everywhere). This saying was passed along by the soldiers, and ever after this, Toussaint was called "Toussaint L'Ouverture" (Toussaint, the opening). 'Tis true he had been in battles and made openings, but nothing terrible had happened to him yet.

For a long time, the French general seemed to have very little confidence in Toussaint, but once this general was thrown into prison on the island, Toussaint marched at the head of an army of 10,000 men, had him released and restored him to his office. For this act, Toussaint

---

[2] Extract from Chapter X of *Unsung Heroes*.

was appointed lieutenant-governor of the island. Later on, he became commander-in-chief of the French army in Santo Domingo. This was the most important position on the island where Toussaint had been a slave for nearly fifty years. Everywhere, people gladly cooperated with him in his administration.

Now that things were going well, he sent his two sons to Paris to be educated. The French rulers publicly praised him and called him the deliverer of Santo Domingo. The French Government presented him with a richly embroidered dress and a suit of superb armour.

Finally Toussaint became president of Hayti for life. It is said that his generals were as obedient to him as children. His soldiers looked upon him as a wonder, and the people generally worshipped him as their deliverer. English officers who fought against him said that he never broke his word.

He was plain in his dress and in all his manners. His dinner often consisted of cakes, fruit and a glass of water. He often jumped on his horse and rode one hundred and fifty miles without rest. Then he would rest for two hours and start out again.

During the last two years of Toussaint's life, a terrible thing happened to him. Napoleon Bonaparte, the ruler of France, because of jealousy, it is said, sent against Toussaint twenty-six warships and a number of transports. On board these vessels, there were twenty-five thousand French soldiers. When Toussaint looked out upon the ocean and caught a glimpse of this great fleet, he said in his native tongue, "All France is coming to Santo Domingo." The soldiers landed and began to slaughter the natives.

Toussaint's two sons, whom he had not seen for several years, were on one of the ships. When they saw their father they ran to meet him. Toussaint could not speak, but he and his sons threw themselves into each other's arms and wept bitterly. The French general, it is said, saw that he could not use these boys to play a trick on their father and thus make him yield to the French. He then said that the boys must be taken back to France. Toussaint stood before his sons with folded arms, saying in the French language, "My children, choose your duty; whatever it be, I shall always love and bless you."

One of the boys said, "I am done with France. I shall fight by your side, Father." The other boy left his father and returned to France. The cruel war continued. Toussaint and his generals with a small body of troops fortified themselves in a mountainous retreat. The French soldiers tried hard for a long time to dislodge them but they could not. Finally Toussaint sent two of his prisoners with a letter to the French General saying that he would make peace.

A few days later, when Toussaint came forth to greet the French general, guns were fired in Toussaint's honour and all heads were bowed as he passed by. Three hundred horsemen with their sabres drawn followed Toussaint to protect him. He and the French General agreed on a plan, but Napoleon Bonaparte declared that Toussaint must be sent as a prisoner to France.

It was difficult to take him as a prisoner and so a trick was played on him. At the giving of a signal, French soldiers sprang upon his guards and disarmed them. Then they bade Toussaint give up his sword. He yielded it in silence and was taken to his own home. A band of French soldiers came during the night and forced him and his wife to go aboard a French vessel.

On their way to France, Toussaint's cabin door was guarded by soldiers. His wrists were chained together. He was not even permitted to talk with his wife. When his vessel landed at Brest, France, a detachment of soldiers took him to Paris and placed him in prison. Winter soon came on and he was taken to an old castle away up in the Jura Mountains. In this old castle there was a cold, wet dungeon partly underground. He was plunged into this and there he remained for ten months, neglected, humiliated and starved. On the 27th of April, 1803, he was found dead in his dungeon.

To Toussaint L'Ouverture (1803)

Toussaint, the most unhappy Man of Men!
Whether the rural Milk-maid by her cow
Sing in thy hearing, or thy head be now
Pillowed in some deep dungeon's earless den;—
O miserable Chieftain! Where and when
Wilt thou find patience? Yet die not; do thou
Wear rather in thy bonds a cheerful brow:
Though fallen Thyself, never to rise again,
Live and take comfort. Thou has left behind
Powers that will work for thee; air, earth and skies;
There's not a breathing of the common wind
That will forget thee; thou has great allies;
Thy friends are exultations, agonies,
And love, and Man's unconquerable mind.

—William Wordsworth

CRISPUS ATTUCKS
1723-1770[3]

Crispus Attucks was born many years ago, at some place, but nobody in the world seems to know just where. And no one seems to know anything at all about him, or about his people, except that he was a sailor. He received public notice just twice in his lifetime. The first time it was through an advertisement in a Boston newspaper, which came out on the second of October, 1750. The advertisement read:

> Ran away from his master, William Brown of Framingham, on the 30th of September, last, a Molatto-Fellow, about twenty-seven years of age, named Crispus, 6 feet 2 inches high, short curl'd hair, his knees nearer together than common; had on a light colour'd Bearskin Coat, plain brown Fustain [*sic*] Jacket, or brown all-wool one, new Buckskin Breeches, blue yarn stock, and a checked wollen shirt.
>
> Whoever shall take up said Runaway, and convey him to his above said Master, shall have ten pounds, Old Tenor[4] Reward, and all necessary charges paid.
> Boston, Oct. 2, 1750

The name of Crispus Attucks appeared in the Boston newspapers just once more, and that was twenty years later, at the time of the Boston Massacre. In those days Crispus Attucks knew nothing about the United States, and nobody else did, for there were no United States. There were only the American colonies of Great Britain.

Because Great Britain knew that these colonies were angry with her, she sent several regiments of soldiers over to Boston, Massachusetts.

---

[3] Chapter XIII of *Unsung Heroes*.
[4] Paper currency issued by American colonial governments in the eighteenth century. *Webster's Revised Unabridged Dictionary*. S.v. "Old Tenor." Retrieved March 25 2024 from **https://www.thefreedictionary.com/Old+Tenor**

These soldiers were to make the colonies obey England. Everyone in Boston seemed to be speaking against these British soldiers.

Finally a group of men led by Crispus Attucks began to pelt them with missiles and chunks of ice, and to dare them to fire their guns, but the British soldiers fired. Shells from their guns struck Crispus Attucks and three other men. Crispus Attucks and one of the men, by the name of Caldwell, fell dead. The other two were mortally wounded.

The whole city of Boston was in an uproar. Bells were ringing everywhere, and people were running here and there as if they were crazy. In the midst of all of this excitement, the bodies of Crispus Attucks and Caldwell were taken into Faneuil Hall. It is said that their faces were looked upon by the largest gathering of people ever assembled there. One of the men who fell was buried from his mother's home. Another was buried from his brother's home, but Attucks and Caldwell, being strangers in the city, were buried from Faneuil Hall.

The four hearses bearing the bodies of the dead men met in King Street. From there the funeral procession moved in columns six deep. There was an extended line of carriages containing the first citizens of Boston. The four bodies were buried in one grave, and over the grave was placed a stone with this inscription:

> Long as in Freedom's cause the wise contend,
> Dear to your Country shall your fame extend;
> While to the world the lettered stone shall tell
> Where Caldwell, Attucks, Gray and Maverick fell.

Crispus Attucks is sometimes called a madcap, because he led the Boston Massacre charge, which was the beginning of the Revolutionary War. He had apparently been around Boston for some years and had listened to the fiery speeches of some of the orators of that day.

A memorial shaft was later erected on Boston Common to the memory of these men, and a memorial tablet was placed on State Street in Boston.

From the poem read at the dedication of the Crispus Attucks Monument in Boston, November 14, 1888

Where shall we seek for a hero, and where shall we find a story?

Our laurels are wreathed for conquest, our songs for completed glory.

But we honour a shrine unfinished, a column uncapped with pride,

If we sing the deed that was sown like seed when Crispus Attucks died.

***

Haynes's tales of "unsung heroes"—which she calls "stories to read to a little friend"—also include the lives and achievements of Frederick Douglass, Paul Laurence Dunbar, Booker T. Washington, Alexander S. Pushkin, Blanche Kelso Bruce, Samuel Coleridge-Taylor, Benjamin Banneker, Phillis Wheatley, Josiah Henson, Sojourner Truth, Alexandre Dumas, Paul Cuffé, Alexander Crummel, and John Mercer Langston.

AFTERWORD: PALMARES, QUILOMBOS, EGO-HISTORY, AND LEGACIES

The first accounts of Palmares—the most important maroon community in the Americas—date from the late sixteenth century. Over the course of nearly 150 years, thousands of Africans and their descendants formed villages, reinventing cultures, economies, and identities. They resisted Portuguese and Dutch colonial troops, as well as expeditions sent by planters and farmers. Given the difficulty—well-nigh impossibility—of putting an end to the quilombos (in Brazil, they were initially called *mocambos),* the colonial authorities went so far as to propose a peace treaty recognising those communities in exchange for their loyalty to the Portuguese Crown. Ganga-Zumba, the planters, and officials of the Captaincy of Pernambuco came to terms in 1678. However, the inhabitants of Palmares eventually rejected that agreement, primarily because it was sabotaged by planters who coveted the land the maroons occupied in the Serra da Barriga mountains. The repression continued, and Palmares was considered destroyed in 1696 after the murder of Zumbi, its greatest leader.

How did Palmares persist in historical memory? We know nothing about the use of that memory in the grassroots abolitionist struggle at the end of the nineteenth century. There are not many images of it in works by poets like Castro Alves, Luiz Gama, and Cruz e Souza.[1] At the dawn of the twentieth century, workers' newspapers and the so-called Black press did mention Palmares; and there was Black mobilisation in Brazilian cities, gaining prominence through the Frente Negra Brasileira (Black Brazilian Front) and the Teatro Experimental do Negro (Black Experimental Theatre) by means of newspapers, and congresses, conventions, and assemblies held in the 30s to 50s in cities such as Rio de Janeiro, Recife, Salvador, São Paulo, and Santos.

But Palmares, Ganga-Zumba, and particularly Zumbi, would only become symbols of political activism in the last quarter of the twentieth century. Today, the *20th of November*—the date when Zumbi was killed in 1695—is an official holiday in dozens of Brazilian states and hundreds of municipalities thanks to the mobilisation of the Black population and activists in the fight against racial discrimination, which intensified in the twenty-first century. In the 1970s, the poet Oliveira Silveira not only played a decisive role in this more contemporary political reframing but left a record of it in his writings and statements. The tradition of political struggle took on fresh contours for young

---

[1] Antônio Frederico de Castro Alves (1847-1871) and Luís Gonzaga Pinto da Gama (1830-1882) were abolitionists. Castro Alves was mixed race, and Gama and the Symbolist poet João da Cruz e Souza (1861-1898) were Black. Of the three, only Gama had personal experience of living in bondage –Ed.

people during the military dictatorship[2] with the establishment of the Black movement in 1978.

Regarding monuments, the highlight was the so-called Zumbi Memorial in the 1980s. Black activists visited the Serra da Barriga for the first time (in what is now the municipality of União de Palmares, in the State of Alagoas) and proposed transforming the site into a space that represented the fight against racism and racial oppression. The idea gained strength, and in almost every year of that decade, activists went to visit the Serra da Barriga from various parts of Brazil in the month of November. The National Artistic Heritage Institute (IPHAN) listed the site as an historic monument in 1985.

Ten years later, in 1995, several Black social movement entities organised a march in Brasília to commemorate the 300th anniversary of Zumbi's death. On that occasion, they presented a list of demands for the eradication of racism and development of the Black community to the President of the Republic [then Fernando Henrique Cardoso]. In 2003, President Lula visited the Serra da Barriga, where he launched the National Racial Equality Policy. In 2006, the Quilombo dos Palmares Memorial Park was officially opened on that site.

As proposed by Koselleck, the history and memory of the Palmares quilombo in different *layers of time* may have represented and composed complex "horizons of expectations" for generations of Black intellectuals and anti-racist mobilisation. This particularly impacted Black youth in the diaspora, especially in the 70s and 80s. Local events and Atlantic characters (and their African dimension) formed a combination of sounds and images that activated my historical ethnic awareness. To the sound of James Brown, Diana Ross, Marvin Gaye, and others, in the mid-1970s I enjoyed the last phase of soul music dances. Black youth were swept up in a wave of clothing styles, symbols, and aesthetics. In 1979, the dubbed miniseries *Roots* appeared on Brazilian TV, an adaptation of the book by the Black North American

---

[2] The regime that overthrew a democratically elected government in Brazil in 1964 and ended 21 years later –Ed.

author Alex Haley. In the USA, when *Roots* first aired in 1977, it was a phenomenon that attracted millions of viewers. As for Brazil, little is known about its repercussions and impacts there. Haley created a fictional character, Kunta Kinte, born in 1750 in The Gambia, West Africa. Captured in 1767, he was caught up in the web of the transatlantic trade, enslaved, and transported to British America, living in bondage in Maryland.

As for me, the intersection of Black effervescence and the historical reconstruction of African ancestors and slavery was intertwined with the memory of the story (what was known and recounted) of Palmares. It was no coincidence that in 1986, when I enrolled in a public university to study History, I had the opportunity to climb the Serra da Barriga along with several Black activists. It was a repeat of the powerful mobilisation—begun in 1981 and gaining strength between 1984 and 1987—of Black conferences in the North-Northeast, and even more so the local pilgrimage to Palmares. Major Black intellectuals from the diaspora participated. In 1986, the visitors included not only Abdias do Nascimento and other leading Brazilian activists but also Stokely Carmichael.

However, quilombos—beyond Palmares—were never mere symbols. The rural Black communities living in the remnants of quilombos are not just part of the "historical past." They exist and reproduce. They arose from escapes and forms of occupation over hundreds of years, as well as the donation of land to freedpersons since the late eighteenth century, including the migration of Black families and the occupation of land in the last decade of slavery [the late 1870s and 1880s] and the first years of the post-emancipation period.

How the history of Palmares shaped generations of intellectuals is another chapter in history (that of ideas) which needs to be written. The shift of the historiographical focus towards slavery and post-emancipation between the late twentieth century and the present era is well known. Approaches, sources, methodological perspectives, influences, and many other topics for an intellectual history of Brazilian historiography await this chapter. It is always important to highlight the leading role of recent generations—including many Black intellectuals—in studies carried out in the top graduate programmes in various parts of Brazil. It will also be essential to underscore the circumstances of the period when Brazil returned to democracy in the 1980s and 90s, and the role of social movements and public policies to combat racial inequalities, a historiography that has been mobilised to understand varied nuances of a Brazil faced with retentions, legacies, inheritances, and projects of exclusion that reinvented themselves in a country that wanted to be modern in the narratives of white urban sectors.

Flavio Gomes

Fig. 6. Bust of Zumbi dos Palmares in Brasília.

WHO'S WHO OF CONTRIBUTORS

Jessie Redmon Fauset (1882-1961). An editor, poet, and novelist born in Camden County, New Jersey. Shea attended Cornell University and was one of the first Black women to join the Phi Beta Kappa society. As literary editor of *The Crisis,* she helped publish works by Countee Kullen, Claude McKay, Nella Larsen, and Langston Hughes. The Harlem Renaissance began at a party originally intended to launch her novel, *There is Confusion.* She died in Philadelphia, Pennsylvania.

James Mercer Langston Hughes (1901-1967). Considered a leader of the Harlem Renaissance, Langston Hughes was a poet, social activist, novelist, playwright, and columnist. One of his best-known poems, "The Negro Speaks of Rivers," was first published in *The Crisis* in 1921. He was born in Joplin, Missouri, and died in New York City.

Arthur (Arturo) Alfonso Schomburg (1874-1938). Baptized in San Juan, Puerto Rico, in 1874, but probably born in the Virgin Islands, Schomburg emigrated to the United States in 1891. A major participant in the Harlem Renaissance, he accumulated a vast collection of books and documents on the history and culture of Africans and Black Americans which is now housed in the Schomburg Center for Research in Black Culture. He died in New York City.

Helen Sabrina Gledhill (1955-). Sabrina Gledhill is a British scholar, writer, translator, and publisher who focusses on Black Atlantic leaders and intellectuals. Her previous publications include the edited volume *Manuel Querino (1851-1923): An Afro-Brazilian Pioneer in the Age of Scientific Racism.*

William Cooper Nell (1816-1874). An abolitionist and writer born in Boston, Massachusetts, Nell fought school segregation and made valuable contributions to the history of Black soldiers. He died in his home town, having spent some time in Rochester New York, where he published Frederick Douglass's *The North Star.*

George Washington Williams (1849-1891). One of the first Black American historians of Africans and their descendants in the United States, Williams was also a soldier, having fought in the U.S. Civil War and Mexico, a journalist, lawyer, and politician who served in the Ohio House of Representatives from 1880 to 1881. He was born in Bedford Springs, Pennsylvania, and died in Blackpool, England.

Manuel Raymundo Querino (1851-1923). The first Black intellectual to highlight the contributions made to Brazilian society by Africans and their descendants, Manuel Querino was a soldier, militant journalist, abolitionist, politician, folklorist, ethnologist, and art historian, among other activities and interests. He was born in Santo Amaro, in what was then the Brazilian province of Bahia, and died in Salvador, Bahia.

Booker Taliaferro Washington (1856-1915). The founder and first principal of the Tuskegee Institute, Washington became famous around the world for his best-known autobiography, *Up from Slavery,* first published in book form in 1901 and translated into numerous languages. Born into slavery in Hale's Ford, Virginia, he died in his home on the Tuskegee campus in Alabama.

Carter Godwin Woodson (1875-1950). Born in Virginia to a formerly enslaved couple, Carter G. Woodson was the founder of the Association for the Study of African American Life and History and *The Journal of Negro History.* His best-known works include *A Century of Negro Migration* (1918), *The Education of the Negro Prior to 1861* (1919), *The History of the Negro Church* (1921), and *The Negro in Our History* (1922). He died in Washington, D. C.

Joel Augustus Rogers (1880-1966). An author, journalist, and amateur historian, J. A. Rogers was born in Jamaica and emigrated to the United States in 1906. His best-known works include *From "Superman" to Man, 100 Amazing Facts about the Negro, Sex and Race,* and *The World's Great Men of Color.* He died in New York City.

THE NEED FOR HEROES

William Edward Burghardt Du Bois (1868-1963). A sociologist, civil rights activist, and historian born in Great Barrington, Massachusetts, W. E. B. Du Bois co-founded the NAACP and edited its magazine, *The Crisis* for many years. His best-known work is *The Souls of Black Folk,* which has been translated into many languages. In 1963, he became a citizen of Ghana, where he died and was given a state funeral.

Elizabeth Ross Haynes (1883–1953). Born to formerly enslaved parents in Mount Willing Alabama, Haynes became a sociologist and social worker who studied at Fisk and Columbia University. In addition to *Unsung Heroes,* she published a biography of Major Richard Robert Wright, Sr., *The Black Boy of Atlanta.* She died in New York City.

Flavio dos Santos Gomes (1964-). Flavio Gomes is a Brazilian historian and author. His writings include books and articles on maroons published in Portuguese, English, French, and Spanish. The winner of the prestigious Jabuti Prize and a Guggenheim Fellow, he has been a professor of History at the Universidade Federal do Rio de Janeiro (UFRJ) since 1998.

ILLUSTRATIONS

Frontispiece

Memorial to the 54th Massachusetts Regiment by Augustus Saint-Gaudens (detail). National Gallery, Washington, D.C. Photo by Sabrina Gledhill, 2013.

Foreword

Portrait of Arthur (Arturo) Alfonso Schomburg.
Source:
en.wikipedia.org/wiki/Arturo_Alfonso_Schomburg#/media/Fil e:Arturo_Alfonso_Schomburg.jpg

Editor's Introduction

Fig. 1. Statue of Zumbi dos Palmares in Praça da Sé, Salvador, Bahia, Brazil. Photo by Maurício Tesserolli (2013). Reproduced with permission from the photographer.

Chapter 1

Portrait of William Cooper Nell.
Source:
www.theliberatorfiles.com/liberator-photo-gallery/

Crispus Attucks, the First Martyr of the American Revolution, King (now State) Street, Boston, March 5th, 1770. Illustration from *The Colored Patriots of the American Revolution,* p. 16.

Chapter 2

Portrait of George Washington Williams.
Source:
en.wikipedia.org/wiki/George_Washington_Williams#/media/
File:George_W._Williams_from_History_of_Negro_Troops.jpg

Chapter 3

Portrait of Manuel Raymundo Querino.
Source: Calmon, Jorge. *O vereador Manuel Querino*. Salvador: Câmara
Municipal de Salvador, 1995.

Fig. 2. Benin bronze. Collection of the British Museum. Photo by
Sabrina Gledhill (2024).

Chapter 4

Portrait   of   Booker   T.   Washington.   Source:
en.wikipedia.org/wiki/booker_t._washington#/media/file:book
er_t_washington_retouched_flattened-crop.jpg
P. 63 Illustration from *My Larger Education* (!911). Source :
archive.org/details/largereducation00washrich/page/218/mode
/2up

P. 73 Illustration from *My Larger Education* (1911) Source:
archive.org/details/largereducation00washrich/page/234/mode
/2up

Fig. 3. Memorial to Robert Gould Shaw and the Massachusetts 54th
Regiment, by Augustus Saint-Gaudens. Boston Common, Boston
Massachusetts.
Source:
en.wikipedia.org/wiki/robert_gould_shaw_memorial#/media/fi
le:robert_gould_shaw_memorial_(36053).jpg

Chapter 5

Portrait of Dr Carter G. Woodson (1875-1950), Carter G. Woodson Home National Historic Site, 1915. Source: en.wikipedia.org/wiki/Carter_G._Woodson#/media/File:Dr._C arter_G._Woodson_(1875-1950),_Carter_G._Woodson_Home_National_Historic_Site,_1915 ._(18f7565bf62142c0ad7fff83701ca5f6).jpg

Fig. 4. Memorial to Robert Gould Shaw and the Massachusetts 54th Regiment, by Augustus Saint-Gaudens (detail). National Gallery, Washington, D. C. Photo by Sabrina Gledhill (2013).

Chapter 6

Portrait of J. A. Rogers.
Source: www.blackpast.org/african-american-history/rogers-j-1880-1966/

Chapter 7

Portrait of W. E. B. Du Bois. Photo by James E. Purdy, 1907.
Source: en.wikipedia.org/wiki/File:W.E.B._Du_Bois_by_James_E._Pur dy,_1907.jpg

Fig. 5. *La Amistad* (contemporary painting, artist unknown). Source: en.wikipedia.org/wiki/La_Amistad#/media/File:La_Amistad_(ship)_restored.jpg

Chapter 8

Portrait of Elizabeth Ross Haynes.
Source: www.blackpast.org/aah/haynes-elizabeth-ross-1883-1953

Afterword

Photo of Flavio dos Santos Gomes.
Source: **ppghis.historia.ufrj.br/docente/flavio-gomes/**

Fig. 6. Bust of Zumbi dos Palmares in Brasília. The plaque reads: "Black leader of all the races." Source: Agência Brasil. Author: Elza Fiúza/ABr. **en.wikipedia.org/wiki/File:Zumbidospalmares.jpg**

BIBLIOGRAPHY & FURTHER READING

Assunção, Matthias Röhrig. *Capoeira: The History of an Afro-Brazilian Martial Art.* London and New York: Routledge, 2005.

Badawi, Zeinab. *An African History of Africa: From the Dawn of Humanity to Independence.* London: Penguin Random House, 2024.

Chapman, Charles E. "Palmares: The Negro Numantia," *The Journal of Negro History* Vol. 3, No. 1, Jan., 1918, pp. 29-32 www.jstor.org/stable/2713791

Dallas, R. C . *The History of the Maroons.* London: Longman and Rees, 1803. www.google.co.uk/books/edition/The_History_of_the_M aroons/qFw6AAAAcAAJ?hl=en

Duarte, Mônica and Roberto Saba. "The Sabinada Rebellion." *Oxford Research Encyclopedia of Latin American History.* www.academia.edu/43995640/The_Sabinada_Rebellion_In_Oxf ord_Research_Encyclopedia

Du Bois, W. E. B. *The Gift of Black Folk.* Berkeley, CA: Mint Editions, 2021 (originally published in 1924).

Du Bois, W. E. B. *The Souls of Black Folk.* Garden City, NY: Dover Thrift Editions, 2016 (originally published in 1903).

Dyer, Thomas G. *Theodore Roosevelt and the Idea of Race.* Baton Rouge and London: Louisiana State University Press, 1980.

Fauset, Jessie Redmon. *There is Confusion.* Berkeley, CA: Mint Editions, 2021 (originally published in 1924).

Firmin, Anténor. *The Equality of the Human Races: Positivist Anthropology.* Translated by Asselin Charles. Champaign, IL.: The University of Illinois Press, 2002.

Franklin, John Hope. *George Washington Williams: A Biography*. Durham and London: Duke University Press, 1998.

Gates, Jr., Henry Louis. *Black in Latin America*. New York and London: New York University Press, 2011.

Gledhill, Sabrina, ed. *Manuel Querino (1851-1923): An Afro-Brazilian Pioneer in the Age of Scientific Racism*. Crediton: Funmilayo, 2021.

Gledhill, Sabrina, "A Pioneering Afro-Brazilian Ethnologist: The Life and Work of Manuel Querino," in *Bérose - Encyclopédie internationale des histoires de l'anthropologie*, Paris, 2023. **www.berose.fr/article2797.html**

Gobineau, Joseph Arthur Compte de. *Essai sur l'inégalité des races humaines*. 1884. In *Œuvres*. Editions La Bibliothèque Digitale. 1884 (Kindle).

Haynes, Elizabeth Ross. *Unsung Heroes*. New York: Du Bois and Dill, Publishers, 1921.

Hubbell, John T. "Abraham Lincoln and the Recruitment of Black Soldiers." *Journal of the Abraham Lincoln Association,* Michigan, vol. 2, no. 1, 1980.

Hughes, Langston. "The Need for Heroes." *The Crisis,* June 1941, vol. 48, no. 6, pp. 184-185 and 206.

Ianni, Octávio. "Research on Race Relations in Brazil." In Mörner, Magnus, ed. *Race and Class in Latin America*. New York: Columbia University Press, 1970.

Kraay, Hendrick. "'As Terrifying as Unexpected': The Bahian Sabinada 1837-1838." *The Hispanic American Historical Review,* Vol. 72, No. 4 (Nov., 1992), pp. 501-527

Kraay, Hendrik. *Race, State and Armed Forces in Independence-Era Brazil: Bahia, 1790s-1840s*. Stanford, CA: Stanford University Press, 2001.

Lewis, David Leering. *W. E. B. Du Bois: A Biography 1868-1963*. New York: Henry Holt, 2008.

Locke, Alain. *The New Negro: An Interpretation.* Garden City, NY: Dover Thrift Publications, 2021.

Meréje, [João] Rodrigues de. *O problema da raça.* São Paulo: Casa Editorial Paulista, 1934.

Nell, William C. *The Colored Patriots of the American Revolution, with Sketches of Several Distinguished Colored Persons.* Boston: Robert F. Wallcut, 1855. **https://docsouth.unc.edu/neh/nell/nell.html**

Norrell, Robert J. *Up from History: The Life of Booker T. Washington.* Cambridge, Mass.: Harvard University Press, 2011.

Parascandola, Louis J., ed. *J. A. Rogers: Selected Writings.* Knoxville: The University of Tennessee Press, 2023.

Pressman, Lindsay. "How Evolution Was Used to Support Scientific Racism." *The Trinity Papers* (2011 - present) (2017). Trinity College Digital Repository, Hartford, CT. **https://digitalrepository.trincoll.edu/trinitypapers/59**

Querino, Manuel R. *O colono preto como factor da civilização brasileira.* Memória apresentada ao 6º Congresso Brazileiro de Geographuia, reunido em Bello Horizonte. Bahia: Imprensa Official do Estado, 1918.

Querino, Manuel R. *Costumes africanos no Brasil.* Ed. Arthur Ramos. Rio de Janeiro: Civilização Brasileira, 1938.

Querino, Manuel R. "Um baiano ilustre – Veiga Muricy." *Revista do Instituto Geográfico e Histórico da Bahia*, no. 48, 1923, pp. 269-274.

Querino, Manuel R. "Os homens de cor preta na História." *Revista do Instituto Geográfico e Histórico da Bahia*, no. 48, 1923, pp. 353-363.

Querino, Manuel R. *A arte culinária na Bahia.* Salvador: P555 Edições: Tehatro XVIII, 2006 [originally published in 1928].

Reichard-De Cardona, Haydée. *Arturo Alfonso Schomburg: Racial Identity and Afro-Caribbean Cultural Affirmation,* N.p.: Aguadilla, Puerto Rico, 2023.

Reis, João José, *Slave Rebellion in Brazil: The Muslim Uprising of 1835 in Bahia,* translated by Arthur Brakel. Baltimore: Johns Hopkins University Press, 1995.

Reis, João José, and Hendrik Kraay. "'The Tyrant Is Dead!': The Revolt of the Periquitos in Bahia, 1824." *Hispanic American Historical Review* (2009) 89 (3): 399–434. **https://doi.org/10.1215/00182168-2009-001**

Richardson, Heather Cox. *The Death of Reconstruction: Race, Labor and Politics in the Post-Civil War North 1865-1901.* Cambridge, Mass.: Harvard University Press, 2004.

Rogers, Bruce. *The Monument to Robert Gould Shaw.* Boston: Houghton, Mifflin and Co., 1897.
Source: **https://emergingcivilwar.com/2023/07/18/booker-t-washingtons-address/** Accessed through Archive.org

Rogers, J. A. *100 Amazing Facts About the Negro With Complete Proof.* Bronx, NY: Ishi Press International, 2015 (originally published in 1952).

Schama, Simon. *Rough Crossings: Britain, the Slaves and the American Revolution.* London: Vintage, 2009.

Schomburg, Arthur Alfonso. "The Negro Digs Up His Past," in Alain Locke, ed. *The New Negro: An Interpretation.* Garden City, NY: Dover Thrift Publications, 2021, pp. 214-220.

Smith, Joseph, with Francisco Vinhosa. *A History of Brazil, 1500-2000.* London: Longman, 2002.

Washington, Booker T. *Up from Slavery.* Garden City, NY: Dover Thrift Editions, 2000 (originally published in 1901).

Washington, Booker T. *My Larger Education: Being Chapters from My Experience.* Garden City, NY: Doubleday, Page & Company, 1911. **https://archive.org/details/largereducation00washrich/page/n9/mode/2up**

Williams, George Washington. *History of the Negro Race in America from 1619 to 1880: Negroes as Slaves, as Soldiers, and as Citizens.* New York: G. P. Putnam's Sons, 1883.

https://archive.org/details/historynegrorac00willgoog/page/n380/ mode/2up

Woodson, Carter G. *The Negro in Our History.* Washington, DC: The Associated Publishers, Inc. 1922.

Editora **Funmilayo Publishing**

Made in the USA
Monee, IL
22 October 2024

67870202R00125